Bicycle

from Sea to Shining Sea

Cherish your enthusiasm!

Georgia Stashauer

Bicycle

from Sea to Shining Sea

3 Cross Country Bike Tours – USA

by Georgia Glashauser

Cover designed and created by Georgia Glashauser

Author website: http://www.BikeSeaToSea.com

ISBN 1-4120-9979-X

Note for Librarians: A cataloguing record for this book is available from Library and Archives Canada at www.collectionscanada.ca/amicus/index-e.html

ISBN 1-4120-9979-X

9 781412 099790

To those who love bicycling and nature,
I wish you miles and miles
of smiles.

To my readers,
"Thank you."

To my editors —
Janice Walter, Regine Schwab,
Nancy Wallace, Bob Whiting,
Carolyn Fugalli, Melinda Nikfar,
Dan Oates, and Marty Chamberlain,
— I am indebted.
"Thank you."

There is a vitality, a life force, an energy, a quickening that is translated through you into action, and because there is only one of you in all of time, this expression is unique. And if you block it, it will never exist through any other medium, and it will be lost. The world will not have it. It is not your business to determine how good it is nor how valuable nor how it compares with other expressions. It is your business to keep it yours clearly and directly and keep the channel open.

— Martha Graham, modern dance pioneer

"Dancer of the Century"

1998 Time Magazine

Contents

1   As Silly As Bicycling   1

2   The Tour Organizations   5

3   Southern Crossing Experiences   13

4   Northern Crossing Experiences   39

5   Central Crossing Experiences   63

6   Why We Ride   93

7   Adversities   115

8   The Joys   143

9   My Bicycles   175

10 Packing and Planning   185

When we experience moments of ecstasy – in play, in stillness, in art, in sex – they come not as an exception, an accident, but as a taste of what life is meant to be. Why shouldn't we be able to live more and more in ecstasy, if we have the courage to venture out of inertia and imitation into intuition and imagination? Ecstasy is an ideal, a goal, but it can be the expectation of every day. Those times when we are grounded in our body, pure in our heart, clear in our mind, rooted in our soul, and suffused with the spirit of life, are our birthright.

– Gabrielle Roth, Maps to Ecstasy:
Teachings of an Urban Shaman

As Silly As Bicycling

I am addicted to bicycling. Perhaps I should say that I am passionate about bicycling. Bicycling through time and space at a swift twenty-five miles per hour elicits a rapturous delight!

At those speeds on rolling roads, my body often experiences weightlessness. When the road crests, my body surges up; I become weightless and float down as the road descends. The wheels pop into dips in the road surface, abruptly rise back up, and my bike leaps into my arms. Leaning through turns is freeing as I sway from side to side. When a sudden, robust wind surprisingly thrusts me sideways, natural reflexes maintain my upright balance. Those physical sensations invade my psyche, calm my mind's chatter, and soothe my soul.

At a twenty-five mile per hour pace, I can bicycle one hundred miles − or as cyclists say, "a century" − in four hours. I can be continuously on the bike − in the saddle − for two hours before I need to rest and give my muscles a change of activity. Thus, maintaining a twenty-five mile-per-hour pace, I take my first rest stop at fifty miles into the ride. At my next stop, I have completed cycling a century.

I treasure those fast rides, but I have only had a handful of such experiences. The downhill routes just do not continue downhill long enough. The strong winds are rarely at my back. The truth is that without descents or strong tailwinds, my riding abilities move me along at a pokey, yet delightful, average pace of eleven miles per hour. On mornings with flat, smooth roads and no headwinds, I can start out strong and pedal at a faster pace. Twenty miles into the ride, however, I am worn out and return to my normal eleven mile-per-hour pace.

There are many different ways to partake in the bicycling sport. Some race. Lance Armstrong's seven consecutive wins have made the Tour de France known to Americans. Many explore the far reaches of wilderness on mountain bikes. Families enjoy nature and their time together by cycling on trails converted from railways to public pathways (known as Rails-to-Trails) where they are safe from motorized vehicles. Neighbors tootle around on their bikes meeting and greeting others in the community. A few ride tricycles. Occasionally there are tricycles, which are extraordinary, low-slung mechanical marvels. Other riders recline on lounge chairs atop recumbent bicycles. Several cyclists take a week's vacation to pedal across a state. Some take that enthusiasm farther and pedal their bicycles across the United States from sea to shining sea.

I have bicycled across the United States not once, but three times. Each coast-to-coast crossing was with a different bicycle touring organization. In 2002, at the age of forty-seven, I bicycled across the southern route. The following year, I bicycled across the northern tier on "The Big Ride Across America." Two years later, when I was granted some time off work, I jumped at the opportunity to experience the central crossing.

This book is about some of my experiences on those three coast-to-coast crossings. I am an average bicyclist of average fitness. I am certainly not a lean, mean, muscle machine. I always need to lose five to ten pounds. Perhaps if I did lose those pounds, the climbs would be easier. Many bicycling enthusiasts are not motivated to be racers, but love the recreation. I am one of them. I love exploring an area on my bike, and there are always new areas to explore.

There are others who have only started bicycling, but will be advancing their abilities and pleasures associated with the sport. They may explore their communities and visit with neighbors. Some of them will become seasoned cyclists and will take a cycling vacation for a few days to explore a state. Many things in this book apply to all bicycling activities, whether single-day rides or multi-day tours. I believe that cyclists who are doing weeklong, organized tours would be able to bicycle across the United States. I encourage them to arrange their lives to do so.

Perhaps you are thinking of tackling a crossing on your own self-powered two wheels. Insights in this book will help you with preparations, inspiration, and courage to take on that challenge. I answer some of the questions my friends ask about the journeys. Narratives of some of my cross-country bicycling companions are included. These stories explain the motivations; provide encouragement, inspiration, and tips; and present some of the demands to be surmounted. The accounts will also help non-cycling friends relate to the experiences of the coast-to-coast cyclists.

If you are a cyclist, bear with me as I explain things most all cyclists know, such as using SAG to mean "Support And Gear." We call SAG stops the scheduled checkpoints along our route where we meet the SAG vehicle, replenish our hydration, and restock the energy snacks, which we consume as we ride. We commonly refer to tour staff as SAG staff. We also use "sag" as a verb, meaning that we have expended all the energy we care to demand from our exhausted, hot, and sweaty bodies, we are ready to rest from bicycling, and we want to ride in the SAG vehicle to the day's finish.

Competitive cyclists may know many of the tips given throughout this book. For example, there are tips to help with saddle adjustments, cycling shorts, the prevention of saddle sores, and how to easily put a dropped chain back on. In my experience of talking to cycling friends and acquaintances, there are many who do not know these little details and want to know more. Many of these cyclists are courageous and adventurous and will sign up, show up, and take on a coast-to-coast bicycling challenge. This book is for them and also for their friends and family to better understand the long-distance cycling experiences.

We in the United States are blessed to be able to do something as silly as riding a bicycle all day just for fun. If you have not bicycled across the United States in one continuous journey, it is time for you to go. Enjoy the ride. Praise your blessings. Keep on spinning.

The Tour Organizations

The three bicycle touring companies, which I traveled with, completed their Pacific to Atlantic crossings in seven weeks. Each of the organizations provided snacks, sports-aid hydration drinks, support staff, vehicles, a mechanic, and some spare bike parts. Lodgings, breakfasts, and evening meals were provided. The organizations had previously researched the roads. Each day, the cyclists received a printed guide to the next destination with every turn denoted and helpful information along the route. When the riders arrived at each midday checkpoint and at each day's final destination, they had to sign in so that the tour staff had a record of their safe arrival.

At the evening camp or motel, staff set up a white board with valuable information for the day, such as when and where dinner, breakfast, and the daily meeting would be. It would inform of the location and hours, of a swimming pool, a laundry, an Internet café, a library, or a bike shop. Sometimes it would declare someone's birthday. It had congratulatory words of cyclist's accomplishments.

Some of the tour organizers arranged special shows, events, or attractions at various times for the participants. Innumerable sights and experiences along the way leave lasting impressions and treasured memories. Some seem forgotten yet surprisingly surface at later times. Memories of the journeys carried me through drudgeries of daily life, such as sitting in stalled commuter traffic or standing in long checkout lines. For example, someone's opening a candy wrapper flashes me back to the small town of Newport, Washington, where we participated in the Fourth of July parade and pedaled our bikes on Main Street. Another time, a drizzling rain stirs memories from the day when I was cycling on wet mountain roads and was enchanted by the misty fog tumbling into the valleys. I am grateful for the riches from those journeys.

Disney to Disney

My first coast-to-coast tour was with the Tim Kneeland and Associates (TK&A) organization on their Disney-to-Disney Tour. It started at Disneyland in Anaheim, California, crossed the southern tier, and ended forty-eight days later at Disney World in Orlando, Florida. The total distance was 3,190 miles, with six rest days during the tour. We first pedaled to the coast, where we ceremoniously rolled our rear wheels from the Pacific Ocean. Two days before the tour ended in Orlando. We celebrated our cross-country accomplishment by rolling our front wheels into the Atlantic Ocean at Flagler Beach, Florida.

Lodging was half tenting and half motels or hotels. The tenting kept the price down. The motels were a welcome relief. I was glad to have the motel space to organize my gear and bags. The penalty of bringing too much stuff was trying to find the one thing I wanted when I wanted it. The nights when I did not have to crawl out of a tent and walk a block or more to a cold bathroom in the middle of the night, was a blissful respite. Stepping down from a motel bed was much easier on my stiff, achy body than half erecting myself from the tent floor mattress and crawling out through the tent door. Another perk of the indoor accommodations was that I did not have to set up the tent, or take it down, and squeeze the wet thing (wet from the morning dew) into its stuff bag. Air conditioning provided an escape from the summer heat and enabled restful, after-ride naps, and better overnight sound sleeps.

The Big Ride Across America

My second cross-country tour was with the Big Ride Across America, which is an annual fund-raising event for the American Lung Association. We bicycled from Seattle, Washington, where the Puget Sound linked us from the Pacific Ocean. We followed a northern route across the United States to Washington, DC, where the Tidal Basin linked us to the Atlantic Ocean. The total distance was 3,308 miles. There were eight rest days in the tour's total of forty-eight days.

In 2003, after all bike tour expenses were paid, thirty cyclists netted $180,000 for the American Lung Association. To yield that much, we rode a budget tour. We tented every night, except for a few nights of lodging in dorm rooms. There were two of us in each of the dorm rooms, which were in Spokane, Washington; Missoula and Billings, Montana; Rapid City, South Dakota; and Winona, Minnesota. Except for Winona, each of those towns afforded us a rest day. Several dorms did not have air-conditioning and the rooms were sweltering.

On four of our rest days, we settled into our little tent city. Our tents usually baked in the sun during those rest days. There was only one commercial campground, The Pine Country Campground in Belvidere, Illinois, that allowed us to stay with them as a donation to the Lung Association. The Pine Country Campground also donated our dinner that evening in their clubhouse.

Because the Big Ride's purpose was raising maximum charitable funds, the budget did not allow for the high overnight fees charged in the commercial camps. Creative alternate sites had been arranged for us to camp. Sometimes we tented in small public school fields. Often our tent area was in a community park – a space not normally permitted for camping. Shower facilities were sometimes a mile or more away at a community pool, elementary school, or other facility. We had to collect our shower supplies, towel, and camp clothes from our duffels and either bicycle or walk to the shower. Staff would not take us in the support vehicles. Toilet and sink facilities near our tents were often minimal.

We politely referred to several of the camp areas as rustic. At one of them, men and women alternated using the only small, wooden, shower facility co-occupied with spiders and their webs in every nook and cranny. We took a lot of cold showers. After being on the bike all day with several applications of sunscreen over exposed skin, the dirt and grime adhered tenaciously. It was harsh to stay under that cold water long enough to scrub all the grime away. However, we accepted and tolerated the cold showers. The organizers stated that one of the goals for future rides was to ensure that there were no cold showers. We hope that they have achieved that goal.

Sleeping in a tent seemed to go hand in hand with bicycling. The tenting experience contributed to strong social connections. We cluster our tents together in the small grassy area. As we relaxed in our chairs outside our tents, we would talk with one another. We were serenaded to sleep by the crickets and frogs. The sun and the birds cheerfully aroused us to a fresh, new day. Dew was on the ground and on our tents. Because we had slept outside, we were acclimated to the day's weather, which made it easier to gather things and leap into the day. We do not procrastinate setting out into a chilly or wet morning. We know what clothing is most appropriate.

At the end of the day's cycling, we are exhausted and want to sleep soundly through the night. Several cyclists packed twin-size air mattresses, which had a built-in, battery-operated inflation pump, plus a built-in foot pump for maximizing the firmness. Batteries weigh a lot and so do these air mattresses, but the support truck carries them along with the duffels to the next overnight location, so we are not concerned about the weight. A cyclist crossing the country without the luxury of a tour organization would be concerned about weight. Cycling across the United States is hard enough. If we must tent, it is nice to have a comfortable mattress.

Cross Country Challenge

My third crossing was with a company named America by Bicycle on their Cross Country Challenge Tour. This central crossing was a step up for me, because there was no tenting. I did not have to pack or haul a tent, sleeping bag, air mattress, sheets, or towels. My favorite simple pleasure had been a long, hot shower. On this trip, it became soaking in a hot bath. The motels were perfect by having an unending supply of hot water to soothe throbbing leg muscles. After all the cold showers with the previous Big Ride, I lavished in those hot relaxing baths.

As it was the middle of the long daylight hours of summer, I had to pull the heavy curtains of the hotel room to close off the daylight that still wanted to come in at 8:30 pm. I had to settle myself down to sleep by 9:00 pm so that my body acquired the rest it needed to be ready by 5:00 am for another day with many hours on the bike. It seemed crazy to be going to bed so early.

A disadvantage of all motel lodging was that they are scarce in low population areas. In the western and plains states this often meant having to bicycle longer distances each day to reach the next motel. Many days in California, Nevada, and Utah, our tour route was on the shoulders of the interstate highways. The slower pace along rural back roads would have been more pleasant, but those side roads do not have enough daily travelers to sustain the lodging industry. Tenting tours have more flexibility with the daily distances.

We began our tour with the festive ceremony of dipping our wheels into the Pacific Ocean at San Francisco. Fifty-two days later, in Portsmouth, New Hampshire, we triumphantly acclaimed our crossing as we rolled our wheels into the Atlantic Ocean. I did not realize when I signed up or even showed up for the start of the Cross Country Challenge how demanding that bike tour would be. We had only five rest days. We pedaled eleven consecutive and very demanding days before we had our first rest day. The total distance was 3,850 miles, averaging eighty-one miles a day. It is very fitting that some of the cyclists printed T-shirts for the event with a picture of road bike handlebars and the words, "52 Days Behind Bars."

America by Bicycle offers two other more demanding coast-to-coast tours. The Fast America South schedule clips across 2,899 miles from Costa Mesa, California to Savannah, Georgia in twenty-seven days. That tour pedals across nine states averaging 120 miles per day with two rest days. The Fast America Ride is thirty-one days of cycling plus one rest day. Those cyclists pedal 3,440 miles from the Pacific Ocean at Costa Mesa, California across thirteen states, to the Atlantic Ocean in Boston, Massachusetts. America by Bicycle's brochure describes the ride as " ... aggressive and very challenging ... a wild ride ... "

Whew! I will not be signing up for either of those fast coast-to-coast rides. The Cross Country Challenge was at my limit of demanding cycling. That central route was the most difficult of my three crossings.

Southern Crossing

Experiences

The Tim Kneeland and Associates (TK&A) staff made the Southern Crossing journey memorable in many unexpected ways. It was promoted as the Disney-to-Disney Tour, although the Walt Disney organization did not provide endorsement, promotion, sponsorship, nor was connected with it in any way. We started bicycling from the Hampton Inn, one half block from the entrance to Disneyland in Anaheim, California and ended the journey near Disney World at the Clarion Inn Maingate in Orlando, Florida. We convened on Sunday, April 14, 2002 at the Hampton Inn. Forest Roberts, our mechanic, assembled our bikes.

TK&A provided a fabulous banquet dinner. We met Tim Kneeland; Patricia Hansen, our Tour Director; Monica Eddy, Katie

White, and Pierre Carriere, our SAG vehicle drivers; and Rachelle Ralph, our massage therapist. Cyclists introduced themselves and shared why they had come to bicycle across the United States or other insight they chose. KathyJo Zezza of Minneapolis, Minnesota had come to celebrate the year of her fortieth birthday. Bill Looney from Seattle, Washington had come to bond with his twenty-year-old grandson, Michael Whelan and give him a special twenty-first birthday present.

Deluxe Camp Food

After friends, family, and staff took many group photos on tax day, Monday, April 15, we pedaled away in a cool California rain along the Pacific Ocean. For our next two nights we tented at campgrounds along the coast. Our dinners these nights were not like anyone would expect of a camping night. TK&A hired Randy Abbers to prepare the meals at the campgrounds, and this man knows how to please hungry bicyclists. Mouth-watering aromas of grilled chicken and grilled beef spread throughout our camp area as we set up our tents. There was no shortage of chicken, beef, broccoli, cauliflower, potatoes, salad, and for carbo-loading aficionados, spaghetti too. It was all deliciously seasoned.

Out of his humble pickup camper or the modest trailer in tow, Randy constructed his kitchen and catering facilities. He set up an industrial-sized, propane-fired grill for the chicken and beef. Another industrial-sized camp grill steamed the fresh broccoli and cauliflower, boiled the water for the spaghetti, and had another burner to heat the sauce. It was the sound of the gasoline-powered blender, however, that pulled our attention to Randy's cooking area. How many campers do you know who carry a gas-powered blender? Out of the carafes poured perfectly frothy margaritas. Wahoo! Party! We were cycling with a group that likes to have fun. It was a wonderful accent for the good times at our Pacific Coast campground and a perfect way to begin our Southwest experience.

Plenty to Eat

Through years of leading tours on this crossing, Tim Kneeland had established friendships and business relationships that provided food, services, and hospitality. They had become personal friends, and they looked forward to having the cyclists come through their area. They welcomed us with great friendliness and hospitality, which was evident in the family-feel of the service and the tastiness of the food they provided. The welcoming, pleasant, smiling service often made us think we were celebrities. The servers would ensure our drinks were full and that we had enough to eat. It was another opportunity to meet, greet, and talk with the local people in the remote lands that we were exploring. We were impressed by the bounty and tastiness of the breakfasts and dinner feasts.

Every evening meal included dessert. On the applicable days, TK&A would present a fancy birthday cake with the cyclist's name.

With the candles burning, we would sing and celebrate that cyclist's special day. We had specially decorated cakes to mark our pedaling 1000, 2000, and 3000 miles and of surmounting particularly difficult passages. Staff put extra effort into acquiring those unique cakes at the appropriate times.

Because the meals were special dining experiences with very tasty food, we all soon realized that we were not going to lose weight on this crossing. From special catering in hotel banquet facilities, to side rooms of restaurants, to gourmet dinners at campsites, there was always plenty of food, and it was delicious.

At the end of the cycling day into San Antonio, TK&A arranged and provided dinner for us on an outdoor patio restaurant along the River Walk. After dinner we strolled through town on the pleasant walk along the San Antonio River.

In New Orleans, we had two rest days. Dinner was provided on Saturday, the day we arrived and again on Monday, the night before we continued our ride east. That Monday, we ate at a funky, Cajun restaurant. As we dined, band members began setting up on the stage. Soon the instrumental, rhythmic successions reverberated through us as the festive New Orleans band found their groove. After dinner we were energized by the lively music and filled the dance floor.

Along the journey, the staff encouraged us to visit local restaurants to purchase our lunches. That provided a valuable rest for us along the daily rides. It enabled us to talk with local folks to better understand the lives and times of people living along these back roads. TK&A had extensively researched the areas along the journey before the organized tour. Tim had explored most every community intimately by bicycle. He had created routes that took us through neighborhoods and along less traveled secondary roads with only light, local traffic. Staff repeatedly reminded us that we were on vacation, and we did not have to rush to be to the next overnight destination. They told us that they would be out with us every day, as long as we were. They said, "Slow down!" or, "Smell the roses!" or sometimes, "Talk to the local folks!" or encouraged us with, "Have fun!" and often, "You are on vacation!"

Chalking

Two of the support staff, Monica Eddy from Edmonds, Washington and Katie White from Kingwood, Texas, would write and draw on the blacktop with multiple colors of chalk. The encouraging images and words that they chalked for the approaching cyclists were often works of art. There were large colorful birthday cakes with candles for recognition of a cyclist's birthday. Other days, we saw drawings of cyclists on mountainsides mimicking us as we climbed. There was a chalking of a fisherman with a giant fish when we neared the Gulf Coast. Every day there were many drawings of Mickey Mouse, since this was the Disney-to-Disney Tour. There was chalking of encouragement, "Look how far you have climbed!" or, "You are an animal!" or, "You are doing it!"

Because they were also cyclists, they knew how to effectively chalk so that cyclists could easily and swiftly read it. The words and drawings were always pressed thickly, colorfully, brightly, and boldly into the asphalt. It was always large, written one word per line, bottom to top, spread far apart so that cyclists could easily read and comprehend each word and phrase as they rolled over the top of it. It took a bit of time, lots of tubs of chalk, and at times, some bloody fingers to press those images and words boldly into the road surface. Each of our names was written at different times making the tour and staff personally ours.

Freeway

On several days of our journey across California and western Texas, our route was very close to the Mexican border. We often pedaled on roads just two miles from Mexico. On my third day of the journey, I was cycling slowly up a steep, twisty California road. I was one of the slowest riders on that trip, especially on the climbs with my recumbent bicycle. As I was bicycling alone, painstakingly pressing my recumbent pedals up the climb, I approached a driveway entrance. Three rural mailboxes marked that homes were somewhere near. A fellow in dark pants and a dark blue shirt with black, slickly greased hair came toward me. As he approached me, he said, "… is freeway?" With a fear of being attacked, I mustered some energy to pedal my bicycle uphill faster. I smiled and gleefully rattled off, "We are bicycling to Florida."

Later, I concluded that the fellow probably had no clue about what I had said. Perhaps he comprehended the word Florida. Maybe not. He had probably just crossed the border from Mexico. He may have thought that the twisting mountain road was the freeway. It did have a good, smooth, consistent blacktop surface. He may have had no idea what an American freeway actually is. It is a good bet that he did not understand English, and my statement about Florida must have been truly confusing to him. He was probably more afraid of me and the possibility that he would be deported back to Mexico, than I needed to be fearful of being attacked by him.

Apparently, the goal for Mexican border crossers is to reach the freeway. There they can hide away on an eighteen-wheeler, which will remove them from the border with its many uniformed patrol personnel and their clearly marked official vehicles. Two days later, I saw two other dark-haired fellows, similarly dressed in dark clothing, high up on a hillside to my right. They were scrambling across the arid land, crouching from scraggly bush to scraggly bush, carrying their milk jugs, filled with water, probably trying to reach the freeway. Gives a whole new meaning to the word "freeway," doesn't it?

Sandbox

On the fifth day of the journey, we crossed California's Imperial

Sand Dunes, also known as the Algodones Dunes. It was like cycling into an unending sand box. We biked across some earthly dividing line where the land on the left, on the right, and ahead became nothing, but fine, white sand. There was no vegetation, but only dunes and undulating hills of continuous white sand designed by the wind. While we were there, the wind was not strong, but enough to make me know that I would not want to be sand blasted there during stronger winds. Sinuous, wind-swept, fine, white sand stretched off to the horizon. We pedaled into it, climbed it, and contemplated the mystery of these many miles of continuous white, sand dunes so far from any ocean.

Juarez, Mexico

On our fourteenth day, we were motivated to pedal our sixty-five miles from Las Cruces, New Mexico to arrive at our hotel in El Paso, Texas as early as feasible. There, we quickly showered and dressed in our street clothes to go out for dinner. TK&A had arranged a deluxe, fully equipped, tour bus to transport us. Our local bus driver was proud of his hometown and gave us an unplanned, special tour.

He drove up a twisty mountain road; we were impressed that he would take such a big motor coach up there. From this surrounding mountaintop, we could overlook miles and miles of El Paso and across the Rio Grande, Juarez, Mexico. We could see the red, green, and white Mexican flag fluttering proudly on the south side of the river and the red and white striped, and star-spangled blue, United States flag waving proudly on the north side. Our driver filled us in on statistics: the population of El Paso: 700,000; the population of Juarez: 2.2 million. After walking to the far edge of the mountain rocks, observing the best view, and capturing our memories on film or digital media, we gathered back into the coach. Our driver proceeded to take us across the Rio Grande to our dinner show in Juarez. There we had another feast with tasty, authentic Mexican food, thoughtfully presented and accented with standing taquito placements. The large quantities of food satisfied all hungry cyclists.

Next, the emcee, along with the mariachi band assembled on the balcony, commanded our attention. To acclimate us to this traditional Mexican show, they started with a cockfight. Two of our cyclists, Dave Wacker of Washington, New Jersey and Art Barrett of Marceline, Missouri were invited to come to the stage in the center of the surrounding audience. Each was given a rooster. Somehow, they understood the rules given by the Spanish speaking emcee. They thrust their roosters into the ring and prodded them on. There was a flurry of feathers, claws, beaks, wings, and lots of encouragement on stage and off. This was not a betting event, however, so the fight was kept mild and bloodless. Dave's bird was declared the winner. The master of ceremonies spoke everything in Spanish. This was not a special show for us Gringos. We were, after all, in Mexico, and this was local Saturday night entertainment in Juarez.

A stream of performers (guitarists, violinists, vocalists, and dancers) charmed everyone with their talent. The women wore flowing traditional dresses in vivid red, rich blue, or bright gold. The men wore traditional suits with bow ties and ornately jeweled, broad-brimmed sombreros. Several performers awed us with lasso dancing. After we saw the talents of the solo performers, the multiple performers further impressed us. Standing back to back, while the woman strummed the guitar that the man held in front of her. At the same time, the man bowed the violin that she held in front of him. Multiple performers mystified us with their lasso dancing as they stepped flawlessly in and out of one another's swirling hoops. Theatrical performances followed with shows depicting the wild deer, mountain lions, tribal natives, and the hunt. It was a stunning show, never expected, and a memorable surprise.

Angie's Restaurant

Our sixteenth day of cycling was to Fort Hancock, Texas, a short forty-nine miles east of El Paso. This west Texas area is one of those huge sections of the United States that is mostly harsh, arid land. The Fort Hancock Motel was very old and very small; our tour group filled the entire motel. Rather than our usual two people in a room, we squeezed three into the room. It was the only lodging available in that area. It is probably because of its location along Interstate-10 that it is able to financially survive. The motel staff was friendly, the showers were hot, and we were lodging inside on beds, with a bathroom only steps away. We did not have to put up a tent. After all the demands of cycling and the obstacles that we had already overcome, the place was fine.

We walked across the street to eat at Angie's Restaurant, the only restaurant in the area. The bed of a large American pick up truck parked outside was lined with dried, white cattle skulls – horns and all. This is valuable cargo from these arid lands shipped to people in the city, who create their home designs with a southwest theme. There were a few local people inside. The friendly staff, including  Angie, welcomed us and seated us in the side room. As soon as we all had arrived and received our drinks, they invited us to come to the buffet that had been prepared just for us. The foil was removed from the industrial-size trays of aromatic, authentic Mexican preparations. The presentation, tastiness, and quantity of the food were exceptional. We piled up our plates. Everyone had plenty to eat and attested to its excellent flavor. We were all completely satiated and impressed.

Next we were invited to come outside to the parking lot, where many folding chairs had been set up for us and for several local folks, who had now gathered outside. We were delighted by the innocence of local children performing traditional, colorful dances from "the old country," Mexico. The children were of the ages of eight to twelve years. The girls wore traditional, long, flowing dresses of either rich turquoise, vibrant fuchsia, or bold gold. Each beautiful flowing dress was accented around the bottom with ribbons of glimmering green, rich red, royal blue, brilliant white, and deep purple. Additional ribbons and ruffles elegantly trimmed the bodices.

As the girls swirled and stepped to the music, they moved their arms in smooth motions, and with their fingers in loops in their dresses, they glided their colorful garments in a melodic, flowing presentation. Each of the girls had their hair tied back into a smooth bun, which was elegantly decorated with flowers. It was the happy, exuberant smiles of the girls that made it even more of a joy to watch. Their innocent, sweet faces, and gleeful smiles were evidence that they lived in loving homes and were exceedingly delighted to be there dancing for us. After the girls delighted us with their cheerful presentations, the boys joined them. Typical of boys of that age, most of them appeared somewhat reluctant to be "dancing," yet they performed their steps and added to the expression of this traditional artful dance. The boys wore tight, black pants, cowboy boots, and bright white shirts. They each had a colorful bow tie that matched one of the young girls' dresses. Their large, black sombreros, trimmed with gold braid, completed the traditional look.

It was a perfectly upbeat, inspiring finale to another memorable day bicycling across America. This is the kind of special entertainment that the local people presented to us because of the special bond of friendship that Tim Kneeland had established with them through the years.

West Texas Rough Roads

The blacktop highway access in this country is an astounding accomplishment of our nation and a gift to bicycle on. We left the Pacific Coast at San Diego and climbed the mountains of southern California on smooth, low-traffic back roads. After cycling along miles of uniquely Arizona Saguaro cactus, we climbed ribbons of switchbacks, which I loved looking down on, as the roadway appears to cross over itself several times. The smooth roads and switchbacks made the climb surmountable, even for me on the recumbent bicycle.

Our route across New Mexico climbed on Highway 152 from Silver City across Emory Pass at 8,228 feet to Kingston. The road was smooth, twisty, and brutally steep. This monstrous wooded ascent across the Mimbres Mountains of the southeast corner of the Gila National Forest forced the majority of us to retreat into the SAG van, in which we were packed like sardines.

West Texas is a desolate and disheartening area for bicycling. It is a land for rattlesnakes, boulders, and rocks. Texas farms are huge. Any big rush to claim the land is for oil, definitely not for agriculture. It takes hundreds of acres to glean a smattering of vegetation. We bicycled nine days across 634 miles of west Texas, with monotonous views of rocks, boulders, and occasionally scraggly vegetation struggling to survive.

A topographical map clearly shows the high mountain ranges that we climbed as we crossed California, Arizona, and New Mexico. It was not so obvious on the map, but for us, in west Texas, the climbs were not over. Challenging ascents continued in the west Texas hills and were exacerbated by the wretched, granular-asphalt, rough, road surfaces. The chunky asphalt is cheaper and better withstands temperature changes, which is fine for the ranchers in their enormous pick up trucks and super-sized SUVs, but for us it was miserable. To maximize efficiencies, cyclists will gear up and press hard on the pedals to attain a faster speed. That speed can be maintained by gearing down and setting a fast spinning (pedal rotation) pace. When we biked in west Texas, we had to forego this technique. It did not work. The rough road surface made us work for every inch. There was no spinning efficiency.

Swarming Bees

On our eighteenth day of the tour, we bicycled from Van Horn to Fort Davis, Texas, and we climbed Mount Locke. Its elevation is 6,793 feet, and McDonald Observatory is located there. This was the first day that we began to see trees since leaving the forested mountains of New Mexico. It had been a rocky, boring, push from El Paso through Texas hill country. The weather that spring had been up side down. Anomalous, damaging tornados struck the Mid

Atlantic area where they normally never develop. That was when the category F4 tornado (initial National Weather Service reports had categorized it as an F5) killed four and injured 122 as it tore a twenty-four mile long swath through La Plata, Maryland. We advanced on our southern crossing that spring with strong winds every day, uncharacteristically from the Southeast. No predominant westerly winds. For our crossing, we pedaled every day into a headwind.

The heat, the headwinds, and Texas' rough road surface were beating me up. My legs were heavy; it had become too hard to pedal that bike. I was exhausted. I rested several times, but could not recover my strength or energy. All the other cyclists were ahead of me. I could not keep up with any of them. Sixty-seven year old Shirl Kenny from Cedar Rapids, Iowa rode a heavy bike laden with panniers full of whatever delighted her. She always carried a bottle of Pepsi, just because she liked to be able to stop and drink it whenever she wanted. She and I rode together for a while, and she stopped with me a few times. Then I told Shirl to continue. I needed to rest longer and I did not want my exhaustion to detain her.

The grade began to lift into the climb to McDonald Observatory. I was so exhausted. I would rest and then ride again such a short distance. I had to accept that I absolutely could not push the pedals one more stroke. I did not know why I was so exhausted, but it was okay. I would just wait awhile for one of the SAG vans to come by and pick me up. So I waited. I waited and it became hotter. I pedaled ahead another mile to where a few scraggly trees were growing for shade. And I waited. I was patient. Since I was exhausted, I sought a place to lie down. Approximately fifteen feet off the side of the road, I found some shade. The grass was scraggly, coarse, and uncomfortable, but I found a way to tolerate laying down in it. And I waited.

The route ahead was fourteen miles to the top of the pass. The slower cyclists would need three or more hours before they would reach the top. The SAG vans were parked along the climb route providing water, snacks, and support to the cyclists. Pierre was parked half way up, busy cleaning windows and polishing the van as he always did. Katie was at the top. Monica was supporting the lead cyclists down the forward eastern side.

There were very few vehicles on this road, but I thought perhaps I could hitchhike a ride to the top. It was a long time until another car would come. At three different times, I heard a vehicle approaching, but each was traveling west. There was always a long time between the vehicles.

Then I heard the strangest sounding vehicle. It took awhile for me to see it. With sudden, adrenaline-flowing shock, I realized that the sound was a twelve-foot high, six-foot wide, massive swarm of bees. They were crossing the road and coming directly toward me. I jumped up and took off running. They passed ten feet from my bicycle. The queen settled at the edge of the tree I had been shaded by. The swarm was still swirling. I thought, "Oh no, Queen, do not settle on my shiny, yellow bicycle." I hunched in low, with alert fear, into the deafening roar of bee wings, grabbed my bike, and ran back away, grateful to not have any bee stings. Now my adrenaline was going. I was not tired anymore. It was another awesome example of being closely connected with nature and having a splendid experience to remember.

Cosmetology School

We pedaled into San Antonio, Texas on our twenty-fourth day of this southern crossing. Just a block from our Alamo Travelodge motel was a cosmetology school. Several of us took advantage of our rest day here to prim, seek an alternate to helmet hair, and just relax with our friends, while being pampered by the students. Ann Yuhas, creator, owner, and hostess of the Salmon River Bed and Breakfast in Brighton, Oregon took advantage of the talents of the gals at this salon by having her hair done in cornrows. You do not see many blonde, white-skinned, sixty-something, retired female executives with cornrows! She looked great! With our coaxing, Forrest, our mechanic, joined us and had a pedicure. Throughout the tour he bicycled wearing sandals to show off his Forrest green toenails.

Quintana Beach

We entered Texas at its most western edge at El Paso. In both El Paso and in San Antonio we had rest days. East of El Paso and into Del Rio, our route followed the Rio Grande with Mexico to our side. Our progression across Texas required fifteen days of pedaling and with rest days, seventeen nights. Our memories of the giant southern state's size were more notably marked by our day after day of battling headwinds. The headwinds, combined with those miserably rough road surfaces, made for far too many dreadfully long, dull days of hard pedaling. I was so happy when we pitched our tents at the Quintana Beach County Park on the Gulf Coast at Freeport, Texas. I so clearly remember seeing the United States flag being held straight out by that southeast wind. I was so thankful to know that in the morning our route would be turning north and following along the Gulf Coast. I was relieved that we would finally have the ease of a sweet tailwind.

We slept overnight with steady raindrops on our tents. By morning the rain had ceased; the storm front had passed. When I crawled out of that tent and looked again for the glory of that sailing flag, my spirits sunk. Now that the storm had passed, the winds had switched. We had had seventeen days of strong winds blowing from the southeast every single day as we pedaled east. On the very day that our route would have us traveling north, the flag was now being blown straight out toward the south. I could not believe our timing. Instead of having the relief of a helpful tailwind, we had yet another day of pedaling and biting into a strong headwind.

New Orleans Rest Day Times Two

We were glad to have two rest days to explore New Orleans. There is so much to see there. At night, Bourbon Street is a tourist must-see experience. I like the French Quarter's Royal Street and Chartres Street during the day. Stores there are like Cajun art museums. I love the local artists' imagination. The fusion of the French, African, and Caribbean ancestry is expressed in whimsical creations and abstract illusions. The characters of the Fat Tuesday and Mardi Gras festivities are celebrated with feathers, fishnet, wigs, masks, gloves, and ornate garments. Bold, flashy colors depict Zydeco music and mayhem. In one of those stores, a funky alligator saxophone player charmed me.

Musicians liven up the streets with their soulful blues reverberating from a squeezebox, a scrub board, and punctuated by a brass horn. Jackson Square offers its calming gardens and monuments. A ride on the streetcar through the Garden District and a visit to the uniquely New Orleans cemeteries are favorite attractions. The market along the Mississippi offered clothing, food, and numerous other shopping opportunities. The chicory-flavored coffee and beignets were another experience of the local area, which we were fortunate to taste.

Persistence

On our forty-second day we pedaled one hundred one miles from Apalachicola to Perry, Florida. With Florida's marshy forests surrounding it, this is a low-income area. The restaurants and conveniences serving the travelers on highways 19, 27, 221, and 98 sustain Perry. Our overnight lodging was at the Westgate Motel, which is an older motel with ground level doors into each room. The rooms were so small that we had to leave our bicycles locked to the porch posts outside. Dinner that evening was at the Chaparral Steak House, a half-mile walk from the motel.

After dinner that evening, Bill Cooley of Boulder, Colorado swallowed the sickening realization that his bike was gone. Since the 2,842 miles from the start of our tour with no threats to our bicycles, Bill had become complacent. He had not locked his bike. He and the tour staff immediately informed the police. The next day, Bill rode in the SAG van to the next tour destination seventy-three miles east to Old Town, Florida. Bill rented a car there and left our tour in pursuit of his bicycle.

He went to the Police Station where he concluded that they were not doing anything about hunting down his bike. Finding his bike had to be Bill's mission. He went back to the motel in Perry and talked to everyone about it. He went to the restaurant and asked everyone about it. He spent another night at that motel. The next day he continued going to every establishment adjacent to the motel and talked to every person he met asking and informing them about his stolen bicycle. After another night at the motel, he continued his pursuit, asking every person he met about it. He talked to a fellow who was pruning hedges. In poor English, the man told Bill that he had seen a bicycle across the field in a ditch. Bill was on his way, expecting to see another little kid's bike. Abandoned there in perfect condition, not far from the motel, was Bill's $4,000 titanium

Litespeed bicycle.

Bill speculates that a kid took his bike, just to take a bike. The thief probably had no idea how expensive the bike cost. He had not taken it to sell it. He just took it. Bill rejoined us in Flagler Beach and bicycled the final two days of the tour.

Learn from Bill's experience. Your bike is your transportation. Guard it. Lock your bike when you are away from it. In major metropolitan areas you probably should never let it out of your reach. In the smaller, rural towns, a lightweight cable will deter a thief from casually making off with it.

And Much More

There were so many other memorable treats. We rode the vintage, wooden roller coaster in San Diego. We bicycled down the ocean walk along the Pacific Ocean that we see so often on television shows and movies. We rode through the neighborhoods of the homes along the Pacific Ocean. We had the pleasure of bicycling along miles of pristine, preserved Pacific coastal lands. In these days when many people want their private piece of ocean front property, it is truly a treasure to have so much of this coastline protected. We cycled in the mist of the Pacific Ocean pushing up and lumbering over the coastal lands. We saw whales migrating along the coast. Along the southern border of California, we saw a solitary stone home built into the vast miles of landscape with nothing else but boulders surrounding it.

When our coast-to-coast journey had its rest day in San Antonio, we toured the Alamo. We walked and explored most all of San Antonio's River Walk. Along our miles of crossing Texas, we visited many original, Spanish missions, built in the early 1700's, which still serve congregations today. The thick adobe walls and huge, hand-hewn wooden doors on those missions impressed me.

We trembled at feeling our tent floor lift, as nature's power of a tornado came near. We were thankful to be able to take refuge from that tornado. Our adrenaline was pumped and our hearts infused with pride as U.S. military jets roared close over our heads when we bicycled on roads alongside their bases where they were doing touch and go operations. We shared the challenges and the long days of surmounting the climbs. We persevered and pressed to the end through the headwinds. We were thrilled by the swift, exhilarating descents. The experiences of the shared challenges and surmounted obstacles bound our friendships tighter.

The encouragement, purposely and painstakingly written with chalk on our path by TK&A staff, Monica and Katie, is still remembered and treasured. The colorful chalk pictures of Mickey Mouse reminded us that we were on the Disney-to-Disney Tour and provided heart-felt cheer. Often our names were written with the chalk on the blacktop letting us know that we were being thought of.

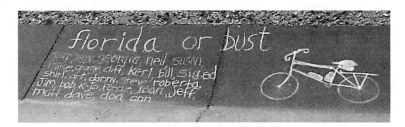

Victory Ride to Disney World

Our forty-eighth and final day of cycling was a distance of sixty-six miles from Orange City to Walt Disney World in Kissimmee, Florida. I pedaled away from our morning camp with Bonnie Mattson from Longview, Washington. The roads were wet. There had been a strong storm throughout the night with intense lightning, thunder, and rain so powerful that it chased almost all of us into a nearby motel. Most of the storm had subsided in the morning, with only a slight drizzle remaining, which soon stopped. In its wake, came extreme Florida humidity along with high temperatures. As the day warmed, we stopped to shed layers. Whatever hills Florida has, our route found them. We pressed on into the rising temperatures.

TK&A had arranged a police escort for the final five miles of the tour in order for us to cycle to the end together. We had to be at the gathering place by 1:00 pm, but Bonnie's energy was fading. I kept encouraging her to press on. We would take breaks, but I would tell her that we could not stay long, and would make her resume cycling. I kept doing the calculations that at the rate that we were cycling and stopping to rest, we would be able to make it just in time. What I did not know was that the distance actually was farther than was noted on the route sheet because road construction created some last minute changes. I was not aware that Monica, in the SAG van, was keeping tabs on where we were and was radioing to the other staff our location and progress.

We barely arrived in time to be in the photos with the group. Bonnie and I had no time to rest. Our entire group bicycled together, each of us wearing our Southern Cross jerseys, which TK&A had given to us. The police blocked off a lane on state route 192 just for us to bicycle on. We pedaled that last five miles together in ecstasy. With many friends and family awaiting our arrival at the Clarion Inn Hotel, jubilant emotions flowed in all of us.

Leap Frog

There were three SAG vans on route with the cyclists every day, and these three staff members kept track of where each cyclist was located. Pierre Carriere of Abbotsford, British Columbia drove the red SAG van, Monica drove the blue one, and Katie drove the gray van. Each van carried water, Gatorade or PowerAde, trail mix, granola bars, bananas, oranges, or other quality snack. They restocked along the tour when large volume grocery stores were available.

These staff were always concerned for the safety of each cyclist. Each morning one of them would drive along the start of the route before cyclists started. About ten miles out, this first van would find a safe place to park where the van would be clearly visible to cyclists. Each SAG driver always had a pen and notepad at their side. As a cyclist passed, the staff would note that the cyclist had come that far on the route.

After several cyclists had time to pedal some distance on the morning route, another of the SAG vans would drive off from the day's start. As they passed each cyclist, they would note who that cyclist was and where on the route they had passed them. This information was shared with the other two SAG van drivers via the amateur radios. The second van would follow the route another ten miles farther from the first van and park. The third van drove along the route forward and back to be available for any cyclist in need. After the last cyclist passed the first stopped van, that van would then leap frog forward beyond the second stopped van.

All the staff were licensed Amateur Radio Operators, and each vehicle had a HAM radio. With these, they would inform one another of where each cyclist was, how it appeared the rider was doing, and whether they were cycling or stopped. The staff could inform one another of the route ahead. When the route presented a long climb, they could adjust the van stops to a shorter number of miles proportionate with the time required by the cyclists to cover the distance. Likewise, on the downhill miles, the vans could be parked farther apart as the cyclist's speed on the descents accelerated and distances passed more quickly. Staff could communicate with one another to adjust their plans – which van was driving the route searching for cyclists and which vans were parked.

They were able to inform one another when any cyclist needed assistance and the extent of that assistance. For flat tires, each van carried a floor pump, which was welcomed in order to easily pump road tires up to the 100-psi pressures. A major repair, such as a broken rear spoke or broken derailleur, for example, needed the expert skills and specialized shop tools of the tour mechanic. That required notifying and arranging for the van with the appropriate tools to relocate and connect with the bicycle in need. The vans would communicate to locate the mechanic, Forrest Roberts from Los Angeles, who was bicycling with us. The nearest van would drive to meet Forrest, and he and his bike would then be driven to where his expertise was required. Thanks to the constant effort of the staff, the system worked extremely well.

Top Notch Professional Staff

The staff on the TK&A Southern Crossing 2002 was absolutely, without doubt, top-notch. Although they worked each day and could not bicycle the crossing, they were all cyclists. Each had done long distance, multi-week tours, so they knew the demands of these crossings and empathized with our challenges. Patricia Hanson from Kent, Washington was the tour director. She drove the U-haul truck carrying our duffels. She drove following the route every day, but made few stops. She was the last to leave the morning overnight lodging area and breakfast service, where she settled accounts and ensured services were paid for. Any cyclist that desired or needed to stay off the bicycle the entire day could ride with her in the U-haul truck. Since she made few stops along the route, she was the first to arrive at the next overnight location. She ensured that the lodging space and food service being provided would be as they were expected. Sometimes she encountered last minute complications, yet cyclists never knew there had been any problems.

The staff amazed me. They were always cheery and encouraging, although it often required a lot of effort on their part to maintain the pleasantness. For instance, one day a weary cyclist came into camp, and when he could not find his duffel, he irately ranted and raved to Katie that staff had lost his bag. Katie located his bag under another duffel. A minute after the irate cyclist stomped away, another cyclist rolled in. Katie swallowed her emotions and the unjustified accusations from the previous cyclist, turned, and with a smile, congratulated the next cyclist for completing the day's difficult ride. None of the staff ever made derogatory remarks or insinuations about a cyclist's abilities.

Some cyclist's actions burdened or worried the staff or lengthened their days. Bill Looney from Seattle, Washington decided one day that it was too hot outside. He was tired of bicycling, so he stopped and went bowling for several hours. He never told staff or any other cyclist where he was. Staff spent hours worrying and driving back and forth, on and off the route, searching for him. Police had no reports of a bicycle accident, yet too many other fearful thoughts worried staff. Seeing their hours of concern until Bill finally resumed his bicycling and was found, made us all realize how much concern and responsibility the staff job has.

When cyclists needed to be told to ride more safely or cautiously, staff spoke to them discreetly, with respect, firmness, and concern.

Staff met every night privately to review how things were going for the cyclists. They were concerned when they thought anyone was not enjoying the tour and worked to make it better for that cyclist. Staff personnel were always the last to go to bed every night and the first to be up every morning. Monica Eddy took a plethora of digital pictures. She made time to sort through them, tag line them, and then sent them to Tim at the office. He would post them to the website so that family and friends could follow along with the cyclist's progress.

There were times when we needed personal or bike supplies. After cycling eighty plus miles, day after day, cycling another three miles to the store and carrying purchases back on the bike required too much effort on our part. Katie or Monica would take us in the vans for supplies. Many touring organizations will not do that. These were always fun social outings. This was another example of the special way that TK&A and the Disney-to-Disney Tour ensured that we were on vacation.

Massage Staff

TK&A also provided a certified massage therapist for the cyclists. Either Rachelle Ralphs from Seattle or Kelly Short from Kennewick, Washington was busy every afternoon and evening helping cyclists loosen up their lactic acid-filled, tight muscles. Cyclists had to pay Rachel or Kelly for each of the massages, but TK&A provided the lodging and food to have these masseuses there every day with the cyclists.

Four Seasons Cycling Events

Tim Kneeland is now offering and operating bicycle tours under the name of Four Seasons Cycling Events. The website address is www.FourSeasonsCyclingEvents.com.

Northern Crossing
Experiences

Rusty Burnwell had initiated the Big Ride Across America event in 1998. With GTE as the major sponsor, 720 cyclists pedaled across the United States on the GTE Big Ride, with the support of 200 tour staff. With new sponsorship in 1999, 137 cyclists pedaled the event. In 2000, the Big Ride had 201 cyclists. Several tractor-trailers traveled with the riders and provided hot showers, toilets, a bicycle repair shop, professional kitchens, catering supplies, food, medical needs, and services staff. All three years, the event lost money. It had become a bicycling party. This was not what the Lung Association desired. They did not want people contributing to their charity so that these cyclists could have a fun, rolling, party. The Big Ride Across America was shut down.

Jeff Schlieper from Vashon Island, Washington had taken on the challenge to resurrect the American Lung Association's Big Ride Across America. He had been part of the Big Ride in previous years, and he wanted to resurrect it. He requested to the American Lung Association of Washington that he do so. They said, "No!" He met with them again and proposed how he would operate and direct it. They said, "No!"

Jeff's professional career had been as regional financial executive with responsibilities for managing multi-billion dollar operations for AT&T, Lucent Technologies. Jeff drew up spreadsheets with many details of how he would operate the Big Ride and how it would make a profit. He would limit the event to thirty cyclists. Much of the tent space would be in community parks, fair grounds, middle schools, or elementary schools. This way the communities could support the Lung Association without actually having to contribute dollars. That eliminated the expensive tent-site fees at commercial campgrounds.

There would be no expensive shower trucks and catering services. His detailed, financial spreadsheet accounted for vehicle rentals, vehicle insurance, event insurance, food, staff, maintenance, and miscellaneous cycling, tenting, and food storage and preparation needs. Costs would be kept to a minimum by having peanut butter and jelly sandwiches for lunch. Jeff argued that many cyclists and racers fuel by peanut butter and jelly sandwiches rather than the more pricey energy snack bars. Many dinners would be cooked by the cyclists in kettles heated on propane-powered camp burners carried in the luggage truck. Evening meals would consist of lots of rice and pasta. The cyclists would prepare breakfast consisting of cereal, oatmeal, and bananas.

This would be a budget coast-to-coast tour. Each cyclist would have to raise a minimum of $5,000 to be permitted to participate. Jeff's detailed budget showed that expenses would be approximately $2,500 per cyclist. Jeff proposed that he could revive the Big Ride and net over $50,000 for the Lung Association. Hesitantly, the board members of the American Lung Association of Washington agreed to let Jeff try it – one time, under close scrutiny. Astrid Berg from Seattle, the Director of the Lung Association of Washington, would be one of the cyclists to ensure that the event was conducted in line with the Lung Association's goals.

Jeff's resurrection of the Big Ride in 2003 was a huge success. The thirty cyclists netted over $180,000 to the American Lung Association. The group of cyclists that rode the Big Ride the following year exceeded that. Those thirty cyclists gave the Lung Association $260,000. The annual event's fundraising has progressively increased, with a $269,000 net donation in 2005, followed by a $275,000 contribution in 2006. Jeff is truly a hero.

Training Ride

Through one of those ironies of fate, three weeks before my second crossing started, I bicycled two weeks with another coast-to-coast tour. My friend, Susan Chapman from Frederick, Maryland, and I had made plans to bicycle the first two weeks of the Northern Crossing Tour offered by Tim Kneeland and Associates (TK&A). We had had such a fun and memorable time on the Southern Crossing Tour and knew that a lot of the pleasure was due to the efforts of the TK&A staff. We had planned two weeks in June to rejoin those staff persons for our 2003 vacation. In November, seven months before its start, we had made our payments for the next summer's tour. The following February, I received the unexpected notice of my part in my employer's reduction-in-force. I did not want to abandon Susan and cancel out on our two-week vacation tour; besides, the money had already been paid.

As I polished my resume and began surfing for jobs, along came the email from Jeff Schlieper, telling me about the Big Ride Across America. I stared at the calendar with the previously planned vacation period filling the first two weeks of June. I would be in the Seattle area when the Big Ride was scheduled to start on June 23. At length, I concluded that since I was now unemployed, I should do the Big Ride and bicycle across the country again. Coast-to-coast cycling trips require time and money. I now had time, which I would not have if I were working. I determined that I could find a job after the Big Ride and sent in my registration form and payment.

The timing was perfect for the two-week TK&A tour to be an excellent training ride. It conditioned me to do extremely well for my second complete coast-to-coast crossing. After completing those two weeks on the TK&A tour, I had one week of rest, which was ideal for my muscles to recover. The following week, I began again from Seattle, Washington, perfectly strong to bicycle every inch to Washington, DC.

Splendors of Washington

TK&A's route crosses the state of Washington via the town of Skykomish, and then climbs to Stevens Pass at 4,061 feet along Route 2. The descent along the rugged, turbulent Wenatchee River into Leavenworth was exhilarating. The waters are adjacent to the roadway for many miles. The river's thunder, wild turbulence, and water spray, as it plunged over and around boulders, were an awesome spectacle. I stopped several times and marveled at its power. I long to go back and cycle that route again.

The Lake Chelan area was gorgeous. The hillsides were covered with acres and acres of cherry and apple orchards flowing down to the brilliantly clear, cold, and deep waters of the glacial lake. I marveled at so clearly seeing the large fish many feet below the water's surface. I hope someday to see that area again in the early spring when the pink and white orchard blossoms on those many hillsides are stunningly beautiful.

The ride gave us the experience of Washington State's high desert area east of Chief Joseph Dam. I have difficulty being in dry heat. In those areas, I needed to seek water to cool my body temperature. I stopped once to soak in a cattle trough. Another time, I found a meager trickle of a stream where I could get wet to cool down.

Along this desert road, when I was exhausted and dehydrated, Forrest Roberts from Los Angeles assisted me by allowing me to draft behind him (i.e., ride close behind him in the slipstream he created). At this weary time, I stopped concentrating on my cycling; in that brief nanosecond, I collided with Forrest's wheel and I was thrust over my handlebars. On my way through the air, I rammed my ribs into the right break hood of my handlebars. Oh, the pain. I had not broken ribs, but the pain was intense – for weeks. Have sympathy for anyone who bruises his or her ribs. It truly hurts to breathe. And do not make them laugh; that hurts even more. Do not expect a speedy recovery either. It will be many weeks before there is relief from that pain. Yet with the marvel of modern painkillers, I continued to ride and treasure the sights and experiences of Washington, Idaho, and Montana.

Having worked in a start-up company developing products that enabled high-speed Internet access over the electric power lines, I was thrilled to see the monument to our modern development when we bicycled into Grand Coulee, Washington. The Grand Coulee Dam, the largest concrete structure ever built, is the largest producer of hydroelectric power in the United States and is the third largest hydroelectric facility in the world. Built on the Columbia River, its construction began in 1933 for purposes of providing irrigation, eliminating flooding, and generating power. In 1942, power generation became its priority, in order to supply electricity to the Northwest aluminum industry and the nation's needs during World War II. Upstream, the dam forms Lake Roosevelt, which extends 150 miles to the Canadian border. We bicycled past massive electric power distribution switchyards as we approached from the hills west of the dam. The switchyards are supplied from the dam's generators by hundreds of five-inch thick lines with one and one half inch thick oil-impregnated insulation. The eleven 230 kilovolt and the five 500 kilovolt transmission lines leaving the switchyards deliver power to almost all of Washington and much of northern Oregon.

All that electric power had me singing, "Boogie woogie, woogie … You can't see it. It's electric. Boogie woogie, woogie … Ooh, it's shocking. It's electric. Boogie woogie, woogie … You can't hold it. It's electric. Boogie woogie, woogie … You can't do without it. It's electric. Boogie woogie, woogie." (Bunny Wailer, Electric Boogie)

Going to the Sun

The northern crossing route organized by TK&A took the cyclists through Glacier National Park in Montana and on the extraordinary Going to the Sun Road. The date was June 14; the last day before the busy summer tourist season that bicyclists would be permitted on the narrow, twisty road after 11:00 am. We started on the western valley floor and cycled along the crystal clear, deep glacial waters of Lake McDonald. This route rises from 3,153 feet at the lake to 6,646 feet at Logan Pass.

We rolled by the bases of waterfalls as they thundered into the earth and looked up at the water descending from the mountains in the mist far above us. We pedaled on, along switchbacks to the left and right and through tunnels cut into the mountain rock. Our pedaling steadily elevated us as we passed roaring sheets of waterfalls free of the earth on their dive from above. By mid morning we viewed the waterfalls from their centers. Thunderous water was coming from above and crashing far, far below. Along one area of the road, named the Weeping Wall, the water showers over the cliff wall to the edge of the roadway. We pedaled parallel to it and played and cycled in and under it.

As we made our ascent, we occasionally stopped to pull on another layer of clothing, with the temperature dropping as we climbed up to the snowy glacier. Later in the afternoon, the reward of our physical exertions was our being on the glacier where those waterfalls were born. We watched the waterfalls as they disappeared over the edge beginning their magnificent fall. The euphoria of bicycling amid those glorious waterfalls, from their thunderous crash at the bottom, to the powerful sheets of it mid way in the fall, to the beginning of the water's mighty leap at the top, stays with me even still.

Bonding

Danny Kenny from Seattle, Washington had a blast on one of the previous Big Rides and wanted that excitement again. When he heard that the event was resuming in 2003, he persuaded his father, Dennis, also a cyclist, to do the ride with him. Dennis' sister, Margaret Kenny from Edmonds, Washington, affectionately known as Dede, volunteered her services to the Lung Association. She drove her brand new, twenty-four foot RV across the country providing our mid-day checkpoint services every day.

Across the arid grasslands of the plains states, I always welcomed seeing that big RV off in the horizon. Dede always set her chairs in the shade for us to melt our weary bodies into. Often the only available shade was that provided by the RV. Having been contained within the insulated tanks of the RV, the water at the mid-day stop was always chilled. In addition to appreciating all the kind SAG services that she provided, I treasured talking with her. With a PhD in Biochemistry, she was a professor and key researcher in the Department of Laboratory Medicine at the University of Washington. Danny, Dennis, and Dede share wonderful family memories of that cross-country bicycling experience.

Twenty-year-old Dan Hatch from Redmond, Washington wanted to add blond streaks to his wavy brown hair. Danny Kenny was his hairdresser. Dan sat on the floor in the hallway of the dorm in Missoula as Danny pulled strands of Dan's hair through holes in a plastic cap. After Danny applied the color, Dan sat cross-legged relaxing in the sun on the grass of the courtyard reading his book with that silly looking plastic cap on his head while his hair lightened. After washing out the dye, removing the cap, and drying his hair, the final result was that he looked quite stylish.

Mary Mindak from Itasca, Illinois; Joan Machlis from Olympia, Washington; and Astrid Berg from Seattle, Washington met each other on the tour. They bicycled together most every day across the country. They developed close bonds and lasting friendships. Although they live far apart, they have reunited every year to ride a bicycling event together and celebrate their friendship.

Fueling Hungry Bicyclists

On the Big Ride, breakfast, lunch, and dinner were provided. We prepared our own breakfast. A portable camp propane burner enabled boiling water for coffee and oatmeal. Each cyclist had the responsibility two times along the tour to get up at 4:30 am to light the propane burner to begin bringing the ten-gallon kettle of water to a boil. We were thrilled that "Mukilteo," a Seattle-based roaster, donated boxes and boxes of fresh, quality coffee. Cereals, oatmeal, snack cakes, cookies, donuts, oranges, and bananas were plentiful. We had to clean up and store remainders, utensils, tables, etc. in the tote bins and in the truck before leaving camp.

Lunch was peanut butter and jelly sandwiches that we each made for ourselves the night before. Peanut butter and jelly sandwiches provide great bicycling fuel and are inexpensive, but eating them day after day became less appealing. When it was time for some variety, those who could afford the expense, would seek out a local store, deli, or restaurant, often off-route, to purchase an alternate for lunch.

Originally Jeff had planned that the cyclists would prepare the evening meal themselves in camp. Teams of four or five would take their turn at the preparation and clean up activities. The big truck carried bags of rice and pasta, along with large kettles, propane tanks, and industrial camp-grills. There were institutional-size jars of sauce. The bread and salad would be replenished along the route as necessary. There were several large coolers to keep the perishables chilled.

Jeff realized early into the tour, however, that this plan of the cyclists preparing the evening dinner would not work. Several cyclists, like me, needed all the available time in the day just to take down the tent, roll, pack, and load the morning gear, bicycle the average eighty miles, shower, and set up the tent and personal evening gear. There was no extra time for preparing meals. The faster cyclists could not wait that long to eat, and Jeff could not expect the faster cyclists to cook the food every day. Some of them were more interested in obtaining a hot shower and finding a place to go for a beer.

One time we did cook our own pasta dinner. It required a lot of time to prepare and clean up. The time required was too much to schedule into other days. Our evening meal evolved to our eating a lot of pizza delivered to our tent area. A few evening dinners had been reserved for us at restaurants. Other times we were given a ten-dollar bill and sent off to find our own meal.

Fireworks

The Big Ride's fourth overnight camp location was at the school in Odessa, Washington. We were told to put up our tents on the level, very plush, soft green grass of their football field. To avoid puncturing their buried irrigation system, we were asked to not put tent stakes into the grass. Odessa is a small town. The population is under 1,000. This single school is used for all grades, "K" through twelve. In any given year, the senior graduating class usually numbers fewer than twenty. It does not take long in a town this small for every local person to know that bicyclists are in town and spending the night on the football field. Around 2:00 am, the local kids abruptly jolted us from our tents by lighting firecrackers in the midst of our tent city. As her tent is not self-standing, but needs to be supported by stake anchors, Megan Robertson from Seattle, Washington was sleeping on the field, under the stars, in her sleeping bag, sans tent. One of the firecrackers was set off near her head. Stupid kids. Whatever quaint things Odessa has, it is the fireworks that we remember.

Montana

On our eighth day, our route from Thompson Falls to Missoula, Montana followed along many miles of the Clark Fork River. Our smooth, wide-shouldered road, the river, and a train line twisted together through the valley, which was narrow by Montana's scale. We pedaled through a town called Paradise; the beauty of the terrain along that stretch was striking. An approaching train crossed a bridge over the river adding to the exhilaration of being there.

Missoula is the most bicycle friendly city in the United States that I have ever pedaled through. I was on a campus sidewalk straddling my bike with both feet on the ground; I was not in an aggressive stance eager to pedal on. While I was busy digging in my handlebar bag for Blistex, I looked up and saw that two cars on the four-lane street had come to a stop, and a third car was slowing to stop. They were anticipating and allowing me the right of way to cross in the cross walk two feet ahead of me off the curb. I stopped rummaging through my bag, clicked into my pedal, cycled across the crosswalk, and signaled my thanks to each of those vehicle drivers. Farther down a side street and away from any crosswalk, I stopped again to dig out the Blistex that I had bean searching for. Many people bicycle to work in Missoula. There are many small, privately owned shops in town and many health-food grocers and restaurants. I believe almost all cyclists would like spending time in Missoula.

The fifth day of July, our thirteenth day, we bicycled ninety-two miles from Harlowtown to Billings. The morning ride started with a glorious tailwind out of Harlowtown that enabled us to easily cover forty-seven miles. It was blowing hard from behind us on our right side. It was tempting to continue in that windward direction for the entire day; however at the town of Lavina, we had to make a right turn. With this new direction of our route, that wind was now making us work. It was now a strong headwind, blowing from our right front. We received a period of relief when a long freight train paralleled our route blocking the wind. Bummer for us, the train moved much faster than we could; too soon it moved ahead and no longer spared us from that forceful, slowing headwind.

Eventually our route turned left and we had relief from the wind, but now we had to climb. It was a thoroughly rewarding climb, because next we were overlooking Billings. We were on top of the 400-foot high Rimrock Bluffs that define the northern edge of the city; it was spectacular to view the entire city below us.

After Billings we rode a short fifty-two miles east to Hardin, situated on the banks of the Bighorn River. We were now at the edge of the Crow Indian Reservation, which we would cross the next day on our route south into Sheridan, Wyoming. In Hardin, the Big Ride staff gave us a treat by taking us in the van to see and explore the Little Bighorn Battlefield. There we toured the lands where the Northern Plains Indians under the leadership of Sitting Bull, Crazy Horse, and Gall defeated George Armstrong Custer's Seventh Cavalry of the United States Army.

South Dakota

The Big Ride route crossed from Wyoming into the western border of South Dakota. We bicycled through the Black Hills where we saw mountain goats and sheep. None of us saw a bear. In Rapid City we had a rest day. Almost all of us joined together in groups and rented cars, because we wanted to explore Mount Rushmore National Memorial. We rested that day by being tourists traveling in cars and walking only from the parking lots to the tourist sites.

The next stop was the Crazy Horse Memorial. The Native Americans show us how to "tell it on a mountain." The Thunderhead

Mountain carving is a work in progress. A model carving shows the plan to alter the mountain into a depiction of Crazy Horse and the horse he rides.

The project, which started in June 1948, is the work of Korczak Ziolkowski. Korczak died in 1982; his children continue sculpting the mountain. The sculpted head is nine stories high; the face was dedicated in 1998. Federal and state funding has been refused; thus denying the government control of the project's plans or the educational and cultural facility's goals. Visitor fees and donations fund the memorial. There is controversy within the Native American community regarding the memorial. The concern is that the sculpting is pollution of the landscape and is against the very spirit of Crazy Horse. Some think it is an insult to the essence and beliefs of the Native Americans. Others think it is a tribute to them.

The next day, entering the Bad Lands was like bicycling on the moon as the strange rock formations covered larger areas. We pedaled into the dry, arid, scorched desolation, becoming as dehydrated as the land around us. The strange earthen outcroppings seemed to have been brought from another planet.

We bicycled completely across South Dakota to its eastern border and then into Minnesota. Along the miles and miles of open agricultural land, we would occasionally bicycle by a remote store or gas station. Walking into these establishments firmly marked the remote area where we were. Very few people came into the business, because the population density in the area was so low. The store shelves were sparsely stocked with dated products. I thought I had stepped back in time two generations. A dull, monotonous voice from the AM radio droned on and on about bid and ask commodities futures with prices of copper, natural gas, light petrol, heavy petrol, sweet crude, Brent crude, live cattle, feeder cattle, lean hogs, pork bellies, cotton, wheat, coffee, corn, soybeans, soybean oil, soybean meal, barley, etc. This droning ticker tape speculation of products that come from the earth is what mattered to these people, but it was so different from convenience stores in our urban areas. It was an experience to broaden our horizons of how others in these United States live.

Pierre, the capital of South Dakota, is in the center of the state. Megan Robertson from Seattle, Washington and I were determined that we were going to share a motel room there. We needed a reprieve from the tents and expected that, unlike the small rural towns that we had been the previous nights, the capital city would have some lodging facilities. There were lots of motels there, but no rooms for us.

The "Germans from Russia Heritage Society Convention" was in town. Representatives from Canada to New Mexico and from the Mississippi River to the Pacific Ocean had claimed every available bed in this rural capital. The gathering attracted many who came for the fun of the hands-on workshops where they made kraut strudel, cheese knoepfle, dumplings, and kuchen. Many recited in the competition for the prize of the best essay. Several accordion players livened the atmosphere. Many conventioneers came to research through the tables filled with file boxes of genealogy charts and other ancestral records trucked from the headquarters in Bismarck, North Dakota. The event brought these people together to discover their common history, to research their ancestral ties, and to preserve their ethnic heritage.

It was another night in tents for us. At least our camp area was in a pleasant, grassy community park along side the mighty, wide, and beautiful Missouri River.

Minnesota

The thriving community of New Ulm, Minnesota was our destination on our twenty-sixth day. Megan and I linked up that day to cross the ninety miles from Tyler as quickly as practicable. Megan was motivated to arrive early; she had located a spa where she had scheduled a waxing appointment. Megan is strong and has great leverage through her long legs. Motivated as she was, she set a quick pace. Although all I had to do was to stay close behind her in the slipstream she created, even that was work for me. At the SAG stops, we said hello, checked in, refilled our water and Gatorade, and without delay, pedaled on. It was a different experience for me to arrive at the destination so early in the day, and it was nice to have extra time to explore the community.

Our fifth rest day was in New Ulm. German immigrants settled the quaint town, which was named in 1854 by settlers from the Province of Württemberg, Germany, where Ulm is the principal city. Ulm is the birthplace of Albert Einstein. New Ulm takes pride in being the "Polka Capital of the Nation." We joined in with the town's summer German Heritage festivities, where we ate wurst and snitzel, we swirled to the oompah music, and we drank beer with men wearing Lederhosen.

Ohio

One of our highlights in Ohio was spending a night at the Sandusky Bayshore Campground. Several in our group explored heightened excitement at the Cedar Point Amusement Park, which for nine consecutive years has been voted "Best Amusement Park in the World" by Amusement Today magazine. It has sixty-nine rides, including seventeen roller coasters, many of which were record setters when they opened. Several still hold status with other tallest, longest, and fastest roller coasters in the United States. Cedar Point is the second oldest amusement park in North America, and it has retained several vintage amusement rides, including three antique carousels with original wooden animals.

Another highlight was bicycling through downtown Cleveland. Several of us locked our bikes and went in to experience the Rock and Roll Hall of Fame. Songs, performers, and record producers from six decades were well represented with videos, instruments, costumes, theatres, interactive displays, and music throughout. Artists, estates, and collectors loan some of the exhibits and memorabilia for limited periods, replaced by others over time. The maze had us grooving with the Mamas and Papas, Joni Mitchell, Sam Cook, Otis Redding, the Beatles, Elvis, Aretha Franklin, The Temptations, Jerry Lee Lewis, Johnny Cash, Jimi Hendrix, U2, and all the others. We could have spent much more time there. With the revised rhythms of varied eras of rock and roll beating through our consciousness, we pedaled thirty-six more miles to our overnight destination at the Geauga County Fairgrounds in Burton, Ohio.

Many months before the start of the tour, Jeff Schlieper had made reservations for each of the places that we were to spend our nights. Two weeks before the start of the crossing, Jeff called each of the lodging and dining facilities to reconfirm our arrivals. When he called the facility reserved for our night in Newbury, Ohio, the fellow at the other end adamantly said, "Oh No! The Boy Scouts are here then. You cannot be here. The Boy Scouts are here." It did not matter that Jeff had a confirmation number assuring his reservation. The Boy Scouts were going to be there. The fellow said that the Boy Scouts always stay there. Quickly Jeff got the message. This good old boy was not going to move the Boy Scouts, he was not going to share the facility, and he was not going to help Jeff, the villain, who was trying to take the Boy Scouts' space. The message was that whoever Jeff had talked to previously had not entered the information into the official ledger. The Boy Scouts were now there. The confirmation number was useless.

Jeff worried as his many phone calls were not producing alternate lodging. The pressure subsequently eased when he talked with a local bicycling enthusiast who helped Jeff secure the Geauga County Fairgrounds for us to camp in. Jeff still had concerns though, because he had not seen the facilities first-hand, as he had with the other places, when he had previously driven the entire route. But at least he had a place for us to camp. Instead of staying in Newbury, we were now going to stay in Burton. Barely a week before the start of the tour, Jeff had to rewrite the daily route sheets with revised directions into the new overnight town, and also for the next morning leaving the fairgrounds. This is another example of what an enormous task it is to organize one of these coast-to-coast tours.

Pennsylvania

Pennsylvania is known by cross-country cyclists to be one of the most difficult states to pedal across. The Appalachian Mountains never quit. The descents are always too short, and all too quickly we are climbing again. The Big Ride route eased some of the Pennsylvania crossing by traversing many of the most demanding of Pennsylvania's mountains on miles of converted Rails-to-Trails paths. The two primary paths we traveled were the Allegheny Highlands Trail and the Youghiogheny River Trail.

These railroad grades were limited to four percent and definitely made the passage over the Appalachians easier. Gerry Rawlings from Freeland, Washington and I were cycling side by side on the car-width trail, chatting away as usual. While we were moving along at a swift pace on a smooth, flat section of the trail, we quickly rolled up to a very large, brown copperhead snake. It was so huge that it extended across the entire width of the trail. Our adrenaline swelled up immediately. In panic, we were both able to pedal off the sides of the trail, and praying not to fall, we continued past that giant poisonous danger.

The Big Ride route took us to Shanksville and into the site where Flight 93 crashed on September 11, 2001. In 2003, there was no government-funded memorial. There were a few benches and many wood-framed, self-standing walls posted with photos, drawings, poems, and other personal sentiments. Ahead of us was the vast field and near the tree line, the place where the airline had come to earth. Just like that Tuesday on September 11, the day was perfectly clear and calm. Our emotions raced. Words were absent; it was sad and somber. We bicycled away, covered many miles in silence, and each had our personal thoughts.

East of Shanksville we followed much of Pennsylvania's Bike Route "S." Pennsylvania's Department of Transportation has placed clearly marked route signs along the roads to mark their bike routes. Bike route "S" is a scenic route that directed us through many beautiful rural lands. It seemed to take us over many of the mountain ranges via the least strenuous and least brutal passages. I remember looking up at a monstrous climb ahead. A short way up the hill, before the very steepest portion, bike route "S" turned left. The relief at the turn and not having to climb that abrupt ascent made all the other climbs tolerable.

On our forty-fourth night we camped at the Friendship Village in Bedford, Pennsylvania next to the Cannondale Bicycle Factory. Cannondale does not normally allow visitors; however, that evening we were given a private tour. That was a very rare opportunity, but someone with the Lung Association Big Ride had arranged for us.

There were many areas where we were asked not to take photographs to protect the manufacturing processes or to keep the latest designs under wraps. For us, it was special to see the jigs and how the tubes are selected, hand-assembled, welded, hand painted, and detailed.

Our final rest day on the tour was in Gettysburg. There is much to see there, and seeing it on a bicycle is the best. Being on Little Round Top and in Devil's Den and seeing the monuments marking the many military actions changed my perception of those first days of July, 1863. Thoughts of artillery shots ricocheting off the boulders of Devils Den, the encapsulating burning and choking thick gunpowder smoke from the cannons and guns, and the wretched screams of the fallen soldiers brings a comprehension of the intensity and madness of those days of battle.

During the Civil War, armies wanted to fight proudly and honorably. There was a general agreement that the early American Revolutionaries had acted cowardly by hiding in the bushes as they battled against the proud English, who stood in the open field, shoulder-to-shoulder in their bright red coats. Being at the fence in Gettysburg, where the Union soldiers were told, "do not shoot until you see the whites of their eyes," seeing the field before them where Pickett's Charge approached, and visualizing the confederate soldiers, honorably advancing shoulder to shoulder across to that wood fence, elicited an eerie understanding, along with a sense of sadness, for the history of these hallowed grounds.

Coming Home

I think that I had a psychological advantage bicycling into Pennsylvania and Maryland. I grew up in Altoona, Pennsylvania and knew the Appalachian terrain. I now live in Maryland, and I knew that terrain. Throughout the tour I often felt like I was cycling home. Leaving eastern Ohio into Pennsylvania, it seemed even more like I was home. The Appalachian Mountains are a pain to bicycle across. They never stop going up. At least in the Cascades and in the Rockies, we finally reach the summit and the climb is over. In the Appalachians, the downhill ride occurs so quickly and immediately we must work to pedal up another long climb. Our legs, heart, lungs, and body can never rest. The recovery period is never adequate. Yet for me, I knew what to expect in the Appalachians, and I was prepared for it. That expectation helped to make the excursion across the Appalachians tolerable. It is what it is. We pressed on.

Longing For High Tech

These coast-to-coast tours allow the cyclists to clear their minds. The cyclist just shows up and rides. A few long, pedaling days into the tour and day-to-day responsibilities can be comfortably and completely forgotten. In this emptied headspace, we have time to think, reflect, question, and examine the lives that we live.

Some questioned whether the life they were living before the tour is what they wished to return to. On the Big Ride, several cyclists were talking of other things they might do when they returned to their homes after the tour. Some resolved it was time for a better job. Some were going to start their own business. Some were going to do more traveling.

I did not fit their patterns. I was looking forward to returning to work. I wanted that mental stimulation of brainstorming difficult, technical, engineering issues. I missed the fast-paced, start-up environment I had previously been a part of. Listening to other engineers and using my electronic, semiconductor, and telecommunications knowledge to understand the technical problem and add comments contributing to resolutions energized me. When I finished the Big Ride Across America, I was eager to return to a high technology, engineering job, which could challenge my analytic intellect. I longed for those brainstorming sessions where I had to understand and perceive the technical issue and complexity. I was excited to add a valuable contribution to those intricate, engineering conversations.

Comfort of My Own Nest

I have to confess that I have never pedaled every inch of a coast-to-coast tour. I almost did on my second crossing on the Big Ride northern route. I would have done every inch if my bike frame had not broken in Chambersburg, Pennsylvania. I had pedaled it eighty-five miles that day before it gave me the let down. I did not complete thirty-five miles of that day's ride into Gettysburg. Consequently, I pedaled every inch minus thirty-five miles of the total coast-to-coast bicycle tour.

Fortunately, the following day was a rest day at Gettysburg, which is only forty miles north of my home. Larry Noel from LaPorte, Indiana, one of the volunteer Big Ride staff, drove me and my broken bike to my home. Because that day's cycling had been 120 miles, Larry and I arrived to my home late. We were both exhausted and needed to sleep.

The next morning, Larry drove back to Gettysburg. I now had my car and drove to Wheel Base, my local bike shop, in Frederick, Maryland. The owners, Tom and Emily Pepperone, lent me Emily's bicycle for those last two days and the victory ride to Washington, DC.

For two months I had been sleeping in my tent. The unexpected turn of events changed the arrangements to my sleeping in my very comfortable bed in the quiet darkness of my home. It was heaven; the next day I was unbelievably rested. It was sweet to be able to go to my private bathroom. I lavished in the privacy and familiarity of my own shower with endless hot water. In the morning, I did not miss the zipping tents and bags at all.

Before that morning, my intention had been to drive back to Gettysburg and sleep in my tent in the field with everybody else. I had planned that I would leave my car there; I would come back for the car two days later, after the tour. However, one good, restful night in my own bed changed that intention. Instead of driving up that Thursday evening to sleep in the tent, I elected to again sleep at my home, then drive up very early in the morning to join the ride on Friday.

My sister, Melinda Nikfar from Damascus, Maryland, met me in Clarksburg, Maryland where that Friday ride ended. She was able to meet my cross-country cycling friends and get a sense of what my cycling and camping world had been like. She drove me back to Gettysburg to my car. We had not seen each other for the two months that I had been gone, and the drive was perfect to have some time to reconnect.

Again I went home and had another wonderfully, restful sleep in my own nest. The following Saturday morning, again I woke up very early and drove to Clarksburg for the last day ride and victory celebration.

Our tour cycling ended in Washington, DC at the Capitol Reflecting Pool. It was perfect for this fund-raising, cross-country ride to have the United States Capitol as the backdrop for our final celebration. Many of my local friends and family came with cheering signs in support of the fund-raising ride and me. Some of them rode their bikes to the event. After the celebration we biked and toured the National Mall, park, and monuments and then rode to their cars. From there they drove me to my car in Clarksburg. My highest pleasure was having my friends and family sharing the celebration.

The Big Ride Across America

The purpose of the Big Ride Across America is to raise money for the American Lung Association. I recommend the tour. The route is beautiful and it travels on good roads. There were times when we had to bicycle along high-traffic, high-speed routes, but much of the route was on scenic, backcountry roads. The funds raised for the charity are well worth the demands put on the cyclist. The website address is www.CleanAirAdventures.org/big-ride. If that website is no longer active, you could search American Lung Association Big Ride Across America.

Central Crossing

Experiences

5

I had lived for ten years in the San Francisco Bay area. When I began the central crossing in California, I had relaxed and comfortable feelings as I cycled on familiar ground. I had a strong sense that the entire nation was my backyard. The sight of a train with three clean, bright yellow Union Pacific locomotives renewed my faith in the promise of this country. The second was painted with a large fluttering U.S. flag. Whatever it is about the charm of trains, I knew immediately that this cross-country journey was the right thing for me to do. I had been living in the Washington, DC area for too long, where I had been hearing too much of the politics, secrets, and lies. Bicycling across the country was the fix that I needed to renew my pride and gratefulness to be living in the United States.

I chose to bicycle with the Cross Country Challenge tour because it traveled the central tier of the U.S.. Having already bicycled across the southern route and the northern route, I wanted to join a tour that was crossing the central route. From its start at the Pacific Ocean in San Francisco, the route headed east across California, Nevada, Utah, Colorado, and Kansas. In Missouri, it began a northeasterly direction through Illinois, Indiana, Ohio, and into Erie, Pennsylvania. The route continued directly east across New York, then Vermont, and to the Atlantic Ocean in Portsmouth, New Hampshire.

I expected that I would show up at this ride and do just fine, since I was an experienced coast-to-coast cyclist. I disregarded the tour name and did not anticipate that this route was designed to be a challenge. For me, it never was easy. The total distance was 3,812 miles; there were only five non-cycling days. We pedaled eleven consecutive days from San Francisco before we had our first rest day. The route wiggles across the U.S. map, seemingly aiming for the most difficult terrain. I am curious why the route designer did not go through more of Pennsylvania's Appalachian Mountains. That was the only mercy given on this challenge route.

The route through Missouri, where we rode on the roughest, chunkiest, uneven blacktop roads, made us all think of that state simply as misery. Roads that were recently resurfaced were miserably choppy with lumpy blacktop, loose gravel, wet tar, and blotchy, uneven repairs. The roads were never smooth. They do not blacktop the entire roadway. Instead they do ragged, splotched resurfacing with rough transitions between the old and new blacktop. No neat and tidy rectangular, flat patches; just blobs of chunky, granular asphalt pressed out in irregular directions. The new blacktop seems to have been hardened into clumps before it was laid down.

Missouri was also the state that gave us the memorable eighty-two miles from Chillicothe to Kirksville. That day featured continual up, down, up, down, up thirteen percent grade climbs in stifling heat. Several cyclists, even the strong, fast guys, commented that that demanding day in Missouri was the most difficult day of all. They expressed that it was much harder than crossing any of the mountains and harder than the demanding headwinds of Kansas.

Cold Sierra Nevada Mountains

Before joining the Cross Country Challenge, I had worked with the Bike And The Like Touring Company for their Spring Cape Cod Tour. A cold Nor'easter weather pattern covered the North Atlantic region that week. The Atlantic Ocean moisture made the cold harsher, and I had not packed winter clothing for that bitterly numbing weather. That week's experience taught me to pack extra cold weather gear for the central crossing. I packed poly gloves, a balaclava, rain pants, thick Thorlo poly socks, and my full cover cycling shoes, in addition to my Shimano cycling sandals. I had not taken nor needed the extra layers on the previous two coast-to-coast rides.

Even with the Nor'easter experience, I was still not prepared for the bitter cold that the Pacific Ocean can throw at the Sierra Nevada Mountains, even in June. We began the climb into those mountains from Auburn, California in a steady low-visibility rain. Silly me. I thought that it would warm up and stop raining soon. My experience when I lived just south of there in the Silicon Valley was that wet, inclement weather had always stopped as the sun rose and evaporated the moisture. I also thought that since we were climbing, I would warm up.

I had brought a waterproof Gore-Tex jacket, which I mostly use for camping rather than for cycling. With my expectations of warmer, dryer weather for later that day, I had left it packed in my bag on the luggage truck. The rain continued to fall steadily all day. On days of continuous rain, it helps to bring along a dry pair of socks to put on, but I did not bring a pair. I had a pair of winter-weight booties for winter cycling at home, but did not expect to need them for this ride in June. On this one day, I could have used them. The balaclava would have helped if I had had it with me on the bike, rather than packed away in the luggage truck. A shower cap would have helped to hold off the cold wetness, but I did not have one.

Although I thought that the climbing would warm me, the cold rain, the dropping temperatures as we rose in altitude, plus the strengthening storm negated the possible warming. The residual winter snows on the ground further contributed to the numbing cold bicycling that day. I thought that the cold Cape Cod spring had prepared me for unusually cold weather on the Cross Country Challenge, but I did not heed my lesson. Shivering, I humbly accepted a lift in the SAG van, along with many of the other cyclists.

The next day we bicycled from Truckee, California over Mount Rose to Sparks, Nevada. At the 8,991-foot summit of Mount Rose it was snowing. John Clark made a snowman. Having learned from the previous day, we were wearing every extra piece of bicycle clothing that we had or could borrow. Still, the wind chill created by our speed on the seventeen-mile descent pushed the biting cold through our skin to our bones. Our cheeks were icy red. Although we wore gloves, our numb fingers ached to pull the brake levers. The cold stayed in our bodies for miles, even after we reached the hot desert bottom at Sparks. We met up with local cyclists wearing shorts and sleeveless jerseys. Their initial words were to ask us how much snow was at the top of Mount Rose. They knew by all the layers we were wearing that we had just come down from that winter mountain cold. We had gone from mid winter to mid summer in twenty-five minutes.

Nevada

Before I left my home in Maryland for the start of this tour, I had gone to the AAA office for detailed road maps of the planned tour route. I remember the woman at AAA rolling on her desk chair to access maps in the pigeonhole shelves along the wall behind her. I admired her efficiency. She never got off the chair. She looked at my printout of the U.S. map with the tour route marked on it. She commented that it looked like I would be taking Interstate-80 across California, Nevada, and Utah. I replied, "I hope not. I will be on a bicycle." Little did I know how well I would come to know Interstate-80 from the two wheels of my bicycle. We bicycled across parts of California, almost all 400 miles across Nevada, and parts of Utah on Interstate-80.

For miles and miles and miles we put up with being pummeled by the rumble strips that stretched from edge to edge across the shoulder of Nevada's Interstate-80. The gouges in them were deep as they were designed to get the attention of vehicles that drifted off the primary road surface. They certainly had our unfavorable attention. The slow vehicles on this highway were traveling the posted speed limit of eighty miles per hour, and they came by continuously. It was too dangerous to try to time a vehicle's approach in order to swerve around the rumble strips. No matter how annoying and unpleasant, we continuously rumbled over them.

Our eternal vigilance of the road surface was required to swerve around the truck tire debris, which was strewn in large and small chunks across the shoulder of the road. Tiny strands of wire from the metal reinforcement cords acted like one-way, barbed fish hooks and worked their way through our thin bicycle tires to the high-pressure tube inside. We learned to always locate the source of our flats and remove that source so that the repaired tire with the new (or patched) tube did not go flat again from the same source. We carried tweezers or pliers specifically for removing those tenacious, evil wires.

We had a pleasant treat on one day of our Nevada interstate travel experience. The highway construction crews were finishing off a very long distance of smooth, fresh blacktop. We had miles and miles of an entire lane of fresh hardened blacktop for bicycling only. Highway cones separated the traffic away from us. That could have been the best bike lane if not for the noise, fumes, and danger of the speeding cars nearby. Nevertheless, it was a relief not to be pounding across the rumble strips, not having the accumulation of tire flattening debris, and having an entire vehicle lane cordoned off and protecting us from those high-speed vehicles.

In Winnemucca, Nevada we saw the First National Bank where Butch Cassidy and the Sundance Kid, along with the Hole in the Wall Gang, committed their last armed robbery. It was on September 19, 1900. They put a knife to the Bank President's neck and forced him to open the safe. The gang made off with $2,000 in gold coins. They sent a studio portrait of themselves from Mexico in refined new business attire and derby hats along with a thank you for the cash.

Winnemucca also has one of the largest Basque populations in North America. This open range area along the Humboldt River appealed to them for raising sheep. Perhaps they also prefer the isolation. The Basque homeland is an area in Northern Spain and Southwest France, although they claim not to be Spanish or French. They have a reputation for being fierce defenders of their territory and their language. Their unique language, Euskara, has no clear links with any other known language. If traveling through this area, I recommend venturing into the Winnemucca Hotel at 95 S. Bridge Street for genuine Basque cuisine, served family style. There will be plenty to eat at a reasonable price. This is not a tourist establishment, rather a local favorite. The building was built in 1863, has provided shelter for may Basque newcomers, and has much history. We sat at the unique, two-story high, wooden bar and drank draught beer.

It seems like the Bureau of Land Management – otherwise known as BLM, owns most all of Nevada. We saw signs for it everywhere. The ores and minerals in those mountains must be quite valuable. We saw very few homes or farms. Most of the roads were gravel. Across Nevada, there are two primary east-west routes. Route 50 crosses the central section of the state. Interstate-80 swings from Reno at the center of the western edge of the state, to the north, and then east across the northern half of the state.

In the bygone days, the route that the interstate now traverses had the most volume of wagon trains crossing those rugged mountains. That route across Nevada is over 400 miles. The elevation in the lowlands is 4,500 feet. We crossed an 8,930 foot pass, a 6,125 foot pass, and a 7,000 foot pass along with many other demanding climbs and descents. We averaged eighty miles a day. Five days after leaving Reno, we descended into Wendover at the border of Nevada and Utah.

Along the miles and miles of nothing but mountains and BLM signs, our tour-planned rest stops were sometimes at exit ramps. At the stop sign, at the end of the exit ramp, the road to the right or left crossed a cattle guard, and then the road became only gravel. There were no convenience stores and no gas stations. Imagine! A well marked interstate exit ramp that deposits the driver to a gravel road.

From Battle Mountain to Elko, Nevada, we crossed the 6,114-foot Emigrant Pass. We pedaled through the very quiet Carlin Canyon. The interstate had turned the road through the canyon into a dead end for automobiles. It was perfectly scenic and quiet, and with no cars and trucks, very pleasant. The canyon and river valley were filled with colorful, spirited birds also enjoying the quiet. Colorful, wild flowers decorated their playground. Unfortunately, it was only two miles to the dead end. We carried our bicycles across the cement barriers; then we ran across four lanes of Interstate-80, on which we continued east.

We pedaled into Elko on a roadway with very few vehicles. There was a one-mile distance where both sides of the road were covered with thick, marshy, reed grasses. It was delightful to have much lushness after all the bareness of the Nevada Mountains. It was also cooler in that reed grasses area, and it was soothing to pedal through – initially.

Soon however, that sweetness delivered a dose of annoyance. There were gnats everywhere – thick masses of them. We were in the gnat's major metropolis. Whether cycling on the right, center, or left of the road, there was no avoiding them. When we arrived at our overnight motel, we were peppered with gnats glued to our sweaty, sun-screened skin. Yuck!

Utah

We bicycled through hoards of migrating Mormon Crickets. These red-brown two to three inch long katydids do not fly. Mostly they crawl, although occasionally they will hop, and they are constantly moving. It is said that if they are still for too long, the crickets coming from behind will cannibalize them. They are a nightmare to the agriculture of the area. They eat whatever can be grown: wheat, barley, oats, and alfalfa. In Mormon history, seagulls flew in, reduced the ravaging cricket population, and thereby saved the Mormons' crops. Salt Lake City exalts the bird with statues of the winged savior, and the state bird is the seagull, although Utah is 700 miles from the Pacific Ocean.

We entered the west side of Utah at the desert salt flats. We started pedaling very early from Wendover as we wanted to cross the desert before the heat became extreme. Our route was 117 miles that day into Salt Lake City. The salt flats are another area administered by the Bureau of Land Management. There is no development there, except for a few salt production facilities and some military operations. The highway going east crosses straight to the Cedar Mountains. It was another long, hot day bicycling along Interstate-80.

We rode 105 miles that day on the interstate, and I was relieved that it was our last day pedaling on it. Our next cycling day, we traveled southeast away from it. As I-80 approaches Salt Lake City from the west, it travels along the edge of the Great Salt Lake for twenty-eight miles. The large volume of high-speed interstate traffic and many exit and entrance ramps steal the pleasantry of cycling along that massive body of water.

Kathryn Reid of San Diego, California; Tina Reid of San Francisco, California; and Neil Sardiñas of King of Prussia, Pennsylvania received a memorable, but not an enviable, big-bang send off for their final miles of bicycling on I-80. As it passed directly by Kathryn at extreme highway speed, an eighteen-wheeler's tire detonated. The truck with the blowout was in the passing lane; another eighteen-wheeler protected her from the dangerous, shattering impact. Exposed on a bicycle, the potential was alarming. The deadly tire shrapnel did not strike them, although they will long remember the images of that tire exploding and the intense, thunderous detonation occurring frighteningly near to them.

The lands of Utah are unique with their barren landmasses of plateaus terminated by the bluffs and abrupt cliffs that define them. On the fifteenth day of our tour, we pedaled from Price to Green River. It was a short day – only sixty-seven miles of cycling. Although there were climbs and descents, overall we descended from 5,600 feet elevation to 4,050 feet at Green River. We were able to arrive early and Andy Hiroshima from Sacramento, California, our tour director, gave permission for the SAG vans to take us to explore Arches National Park. There we saw one of the puzzling, mysterious masses of splendid lands that Utah and this nation have preserved.

Pebbles

On a bicycle, it could be a long time before arriving at the next public toilet. It is pretty easy, however, to find a secluded cove to tuck into and not be seen by vehicles or other cyclists when it becomes necessary.

On the day that we climbed Monarch Pass, our route coincided with Colorado's Ride-the-Rockies one-week tour. That tour hosted 2,000 cyclists along with many private support vehicles, friends, and family. The elevation of Monarch Pass is 11,312 feet. On the demanding mountain climbs, I had difficulty adjusting to the high altitude where there is less air and oxygen.

I climbed so slowly. With only a double chain-ring, I needed to stop every five minutes for forty seconds to let my heart calm down. I was on this climb for hours. Along here, nature called. Faster cyclists pedaled by me constantly. Where the mountainside came down to the side of the roadway, there were no secluded hiding areas. Along some sections, there were steep drop-offs along both the left and right sides of the road. Finding a secluded spot was getting challenging.

I parked my bike along the guardrail on the right. I expected that most of the other cyclists would look to the right for the parked bike's missing rider. I climbed over the guardrail on the left. From there, I carefully half walked, half slid down the steep, stony grade.

With my heels deeply dug in to keep me from descending farther, I answered that nature call. As I did, I thought how it would be for me to lose my balance and flip forward into a very embarrassing bare-butt tumble. I leaned back; instantly my rump touched the hillside. I am thinking, be done with this vulnerable business. I pulled and stretched those skin huggers back on and climbed up to the level roadway. Back in the saddle. Now what? You know how uncomfortable it is to have a pebble in your shoe. I now had pebbles in my shorts.

Royal Gorge

On our twentieth day from Salida, Colorado, our Ride-The-Rockies comrades headed north as we continued our eastbound trek for ninety-five miles to Pueblo, Colorado. Our ride out of Salida was gorgeous as our route followed the Arkansas River. We easily pedaled on a downhill grade for many miles, while we traveled beside the tumbling water, and watched others in kayaks and rafting boats. The river valley supports homes, various livestock, and cropland farms.

Forty miles out we took a side road, and as we bicycled into very arid and hot backcountry, the number of homes quickly diminished. We had miles of quiet, desolate, and pleasant cycling. Far out into these dry lands, the road became a launching pad. We climbed extremely steep inclines in that dry heat. Our efforts were rewarded when the road crossed Royal Gorge in Canyon City. The long, narrow, one-lane bridge is claimed as the world's highest suspension bridge. More than 1,000 feet directly below and distantly far away from us, was the Arkansas River, which we had pedaled beside that morning and where we had watched other people in kayaks and rafting boats.

Hail Storm

On our twenty-second day, we pedaled 121 miles from Pueblo to Lamar, Colorado. As we pedaled toward Lamar we watched the thickening of an intense prairie thunderstorm as it grew darker and more frightening. Lightning bolts flashed across the sky and discharged to the earth. The thunder exploded more intensely than the strikes. I whispered my prayers as I trembled. Our route had us pedaling directly into it. George Carlson of Minneapolis, Minnesota and Jay Butler of Indianapolis, Indiana were only two miles from the Best Western motel when the storm began pounding them with large hail balls. There was no place to take shelter so they were forced to continue pedaling to the motel. The next day, George modeled his polka dot arms and back where the pounding hail balls developed black and blue bruises.

The storm was so intense that the tour staff forced Tina Reid from San Francisco, California; Kathryn Reid from San Diego, California; and Neil Sardiñas from King of Prussia, Pennsylvania to get into the van, which delivered them to the motel. Tina was furious. She had sat in the van for shelter from the storm, but she did not want to be transported. She had come to this coast-to-coast ride with the intention to bicycle every inch. She was livid that the tour staff was denying her that opportunity because of the storm.

Ultimately, neither the storm nor the staff's concern for the cyclists' safety denied them of their every inch honors. The next morning, Neil and Tina pedaled away early. They bicycled west, back-tracking the storm route, to where they had sought shelter in the van. Not until they pedaled back to that location, did they then turn around to the east. Thus they ensured the integrity of their bicycling every inch from coast to coast. Bravo!

Kansas

Our Cross Country Challenge route took us directly across the center of Kansas (nearly 500 miles) and then up to the northeast corner of the state to St. Joseph, Missouri. Kansas has headwinds and high-rise buildings called grain mills, headwinds, cattle stockyards, and headwinds. We saw the high-rise grain mills many miles before we finally pedaled beside them. We pedaled by huge cattle herds squeezed into close-quarters stockyards where they were plumped up with the feed from the grain mills.

On our twenty-fourth day, we bicycled fifty-two miles from Garden City into Dodge City. Images of Kitty, Matt Dillon, and Gunsmoke were reenacted in a staged production on infamous Front Street. This once vital commercial location on the Sante Fe Trail was renowned for its saloons, cowboys, gamblers, gunfighters, and brothels. Lawlessness was the rule of the town. The term "stinker" was established here in regard to the filthy buffalo hunters and traders that came to the town. This town also became known for its red-light district, where clients found their way to the town's brothels by light from the red caboose lanterns from trains.

On another short day of only sixty-four miles, we pedaled into Abilene, Kansas early enough to explore some of the town. On our way, we bicycled by the Greyhound Dog Racing Hall of Fame just west of town, where we saw many of the sleek animals. Abilene is the childhood home of our thirty-fourth President, Dwight David Eisenhower, and Ike is buried in his "Place of Meditation" adjacent to his child hood home. The Eisenhower Presidential Library is also there.

From 1867 to 1871, the Chisholm Trail from southern Texas terminated in Abilene. Cattle were driven north on the trail. The Kansas Pacific Railway then transported the cattle eastward to the beef markets. At the completion of their three-month cattle drive, the cowboys had time and money to lavish on Abilene's saloons, brothels, and gambling tables. James Butler "Wild Bill" Hickok was the Marshall for eight months in 1871 until he was fired. Abilene's Wild West hey days declined after 1872 when the railroad and the cattle trade moved south to Wichita.

Another boom quietly began thereafter. For fear of ridicule, Abilene's first mayor, T.C. Henry, secretly planted five acres of Minnesota winter wheat in this area, then known as the Great American Desert. The success of that crop spurned his planting of thousands of acres. A few successful years of those wheat crops resulted in T.C. Henry becoming Abilene's first millionaire. The addition of the Mennonite Red Turkey wheat rapidly made Kansas the Breadbasket of the World.

The Museum of Independent Telephony in Abilene tells the story of the success of C.L. Brown's local company growth. In February 1900, Cleyson Leroy Brown connected his first long-distance telephone circuit. The Brown Telephone Company of Abilene quickly became a favored alternate to the Bell Telephone monopoly. Eleven years later, the company consolidated with three other independent telephone companies and became the United Telephone Company. Continued growth lead Brown in 1925 to form United Telephone and Electric (UT&E). UT&E survived the Great Depression and went on to reorganize in 1939 into United Utilities, which became United Telecommunications, Inc in 1972. In 1984 United Telecom began installing fiber optic cable to build its digital transmission network. To reach more customers and farther expand the digital network, in 1986 a partnership was formed between United Telecom and GTE Sprint. Growth continued, and in 1989, United Telecom acquired 80% controlling interest in Sprint. In 1991 they purchased GTE's remaining 20%. The name was then changed from United Telecom to the Sprint Corporation. Not bad for a local

Abilene boy.

The museum's many interactive displays educate and entertain. The museum also features a C.W. Parker steam-driven carousel with rare hand-carved horses that were manufactured in Abilene. Rides on the carousel were offered for $2.

We spent five nights in Kansas – the heartland of our country. The route we took was far from the interstate highways. Without the interstate commerce to support it, there were signs of the heart dying. Businesses were boarded up. Restaurants that were denoted on our daily route sheet as having been available to the cyclists the previous year were closed. Convenience stores were closed. Even homes were empty and boarded up.

The lands of southeastern Colorado are very much like Kansas. On our twenty-second day of the tour, we bicycled 121 miles from Pueblo to Lamar, Colorado. We had three tour-scheduled rest stops that day. I was as hot and dehydrated as the hot, wind-blown soil. We had pedaled 102 miles from our morning start when we arrived at the town of Hasty. We still had to pedal twenty miles farther to our day's final destination in Lamar.

The Mom and Pop local convenience store at Hasty sits just a car's parking distance off Highway 50. I leaned my bicycle against the wall and stepped inside for the relief of the air-conditioning and for cold hydration. My quality, polarized sunglasses helped my eyes adjust from the brilliant sunlight outside to the darker interior light inside this old building. The eyes of three, tall, thin farmers, who were sitting at the long table centered inside the front of the grand room, were already well adjusted to watch me enter. I had to be a completely strange looking person to them – a hot, sweaty, tanned, wet-haired woman, wearing typical tight, colorful, spandex, bicycling clothes. I would love to have known their thoughts at the sight of me. I gave them greetings as I walked in and proceeded to the far end of that long table, pulled back the chair, and sat my exhausted body down. To my left sat a thirteen-year-old, local girl. We talked a bit. I went to the cooler for my cold hydration and sat back down to talk with them. My body heat began to dissipate.

Next I was ready for some potato chips. I guess my sweating had depleted my body's salts; thus I was craving the chips to replace the salts. I had seen the local brand for a few days and knew that they offered Jalapeño flavored chips, which I was now ready for. I walked over to the chip shelves and searched for the Jalapeño flavor. The woman working at the store kindly offered assistance. I told her I wanted the Jalapeño chips and commented that the small empty shelf space was probably where they should be.

She agreed, that is where they probably would be, if the delivery driver would simply take five minutes to pull his truck off the road to deliver them. She told me that the drivers speed by their front door, but do not stop. Once or twice a month they stop, but this small store is not worth their time and money. The small delivery that should have been for them can be offloaded with the volume stop they make at the next large town. The inventory works out the same for the driver and the heartland misses another beat. The heart is dying. Soon another store will never again flip the sign from CLOSED to OPEN.

Three Kernels

Illnesses may be a problem on these rides. One of our cyclists was dealing with a urinary infection. I cringe at the thought of how he pulled those spandex diaper pants on day after day and straddled that saddle for hours. Somewhere in Illinois, I developed a female itch. I had not had anything like that since I was a teenager. A day later it was demanding more of my attention. I was rushing to get in and out of the shower so that my roommate had time for her shower. I bent over to look at this, as though a visual of the redness would do some good. This time it did! Tucked in, trying to take root near my clitoris were three kernels of grain! Ah, the plains states. Amber waves of grain.

Water

They say drink before you are thirsty and eat before you are hungry. I follow that advice, which is another reason why I never lose those extra five to ten pounds. As for water, I often buy a gallon jug of water and pretty much consume it all. I fill my seventy-ounce Camelbak and at least one water bottle. When other cyclists are there, I share the water. When no other cyclists are there, I drink a bunch from the jug. If the day is hot, hot, hot, I will pour some of that water on my head and back. I am a crude being when I am existing out there day after day on my bike in the heat.

Our ride across Illinois was filled with many of those hot, hot days. Even early in the morning, I was quickly dehydrating. I had filled up with water from the overnight hotel. When I began drinking it, I thought, "Yuck! This is awful!" At the next convenience store, I poured it all out. I took advantage of the ice from their soda dispenser. My Camelbak, with the three-inch opening, makes it real easy to pour ice directly into it. In front of me at the fountain was the water dispenser. Oh, how nice! I filled my Camelbak with the water. I pedaled away, thrilled to have had a perfect rest stop. I had used their bathroom and restocked with ice-cold water. Shortly after leaving the store, the intense heat struck me again. I drank from my chilled well. "Yuck! This tastes more disgusting than the earlier junk!" Even cold, it tasted terrible. I pedaled on.

At the next convenience store, I would buy a gallon jug of water. I walked in and walked all around the refrigerated shelves, but saw no gallon jugs of water. I walked back and forth by the floor shelves. I finally found an empty shelf where water normally would have been stocked. The price was $2.59 a gallon and customers willingly paid it, determined by supply and demand. All the water in that region tastes terrible. Typed on a tiny sign at the edge of the shelf was, "Cold water in beer cooler." To the beer cooler I went. "Almost heaven. I'm in heaven." I cannot imagine any other customer ever spending so much time in the beer cooler. I sat down on some cases, opened the jug, and drank. I filled my Camelbak and water bottle, which I had already emptied outside. I just sat there, drinking the nectar from the jug, cooling down and relaxing in the beer cooler. I greeted several local fellows as they came in for their beer. I must have been in there a long time. Tour staff told me later that they had lost me that day. Hot dry weather and crappy-tasting water made this beer cooler a sweet and memorable experience.

Indiana

Our thirty-seventh day of cycling was in Indiana and was packed with exciting stops and sights to see. In Brownsburg, we toured the C.F. Roark Company's bicycle design and production facility. Each of these titanium bicycles is hand made specifically for its owner. At the customer's request, many of these custom bicycles are fitted with titanium S&S couplers, each weighing only 300 grams. The bicycles are designed to use 700c wheel sets, yet quickly and easily fold and fit into a 26"x26"x10" hard shell suitcase. Dale Crockett from Tucson, Arizona was one of our cyclists riding a Roark, and he was one of our fastest cyclists.

At fifty-two miles, our adrenaline surged as NASCAR vehicles roared down from above us, which prompted us to pedal faster to the entrance of the Indianapolis Motor Speedway, proceed underneath the track, and ride into the infield. The size of the speedway was impressive. The infield spectator capacity is 400,000, and it seats 250,000. It was our good fortune that the cars were practicing on the two and a half mile banked speedway while we were there. The thunder as they passed our location was exhilarating. They moved so fast that most of us could not make our digital cameras capture them. Only because they ended practice, did our excitement settle and we continued on our route.

At fifty-six miles we came to the Major Taylor Velodrome. Marshall Walter Taylor was born in 1878. He was nicknamed Major when the teenager performed bicycle stunts wearing a military uniform that his employer had given to him to wear for the show. In Indiana at seventeen, he unofficially broke two of track cycling's world records. Because his skin was black, he was banned from the actual U.S. competitions. He went to Europe and by 1898 claimed seven world records. In 1901, he had competed at every significant European cycle track, where he won over almost every European champion. Of fifty-four events, he won forty-two. Although a world champion and popular idol in Europe and Australia, as a black man, he was excluded from racing in many U.S. cities. Marshall Taylor died in 1932. With donations from Frank Schwinn of the Schwinn Bicycle Company and others, the velodrome was built in 1982 and named to commemorate Major Taylor.

The twenty-eight degree, banked, concrete track gave us appreciation of the speeds the racing, single-speed, track bikes attain. Even the straights of the track are banked at nine degrees. It was scary for me to ride on the steep track, but I was there. I had to ride at least a few laps.

We ended this sixty-three mile day in downtown Indianapolis, just two blocks from the Soldiers and Sailors Monument. Several of us recalled the sights and events of the day as we relaxed at the outdoor sidewalk cafes savoring Starbucks coffee or ice cream or both.

Red Neck Smile

It had been thirty-nine days of bicycling since we had left San Francisco. Our dinner that evening was at Ryan's Steakhouse Buffet in Richmond, Indiana. My culinary tastes must be those of a spoiled cosmopolitan. I thought the food was awful. There were so many choices, but everything that I tasted did not appeal to me. The head lettuce was wilted. The green beans were boiled bland. Everything I tasted was way too salty. The beef was gristly and tough. The corn tasted like salted paper. With a bite into a piece of chicken, I received a swell of sensations. With a chewing grind, I bit into something way too hard, and my tongue felt the gap of the missing tooth in my smile. The depression of the crappy food switched to panic at having a missing tooth gap in my smile. I wrapped the renegade tooth in a napkin and glumly accepted that I would have to find a dentist to renew my sophisticated smile.

White Turkey

We bicycled 367 miles across Ohio in four days. Much of our route followed the Cardinal Trail Bike Route, which traveled through farmland on low-traffic, back roads, and skirted by almost all the towns. There were times, however, when we wished the route went into some of the communities, because we needed a con... store to restock our hydration or wanted a deli or restaurant for substantial food. Sports or energy bars, trail mix, and snacks just do not cut it for lunch when we are cycling eighty-five miles day after day. We needed real, solid food! Just one mile before we crossed into Pennsylvania, we received the best reward for that Ohio crossing when we came to the White Turkey Drive-In at Conneaut.

Eddie and Marge Tuttle's family business was raising White Holland Turkeys; in 1952, they opened their White Turkey Drive-In. This preserved gem is one of the original Richardson's Root Beer stands. Richardson's originated in Rochester, New York in the 1940's. The drive-in is now owned and operated by their son, Gary, and his wife, Peggy. They continue to raise White Holland Turkeys, which keeps them busy through the winter months with preparations for the delicious turkey sandwiches, which are served during the busy summer season. The root beer floats were another specialty that we savored as we sat at their cheery, brightly painted, outdoor counter, reliving the 1950's with songs such as, "Blue Suede Shoes," "Blueberry Hill," "No Particular Place to Go," and "Be Bop A Lula."

If it is summer and you are traveling Interstate-90 across the Pennsylvania-Ohio border, I recommend that you take exit 241, north to U.S. Route 20, and savor a feast at the White Turkey Drive-In.

New York

On our forty-fifth day, we bicycled a nearly flat eighty-two miles along Lake Erie from Erie, Pennsylvania to Hamburg, New York. We quickly showered and put on our street clothes. Our America by Bicycle staff was driving us in the vans to visit the Pedaling History Bicycle Museum. When you travel near the Buffalo, New York region, be sure to visit this place. Displays show numerous automotive innovations that were initially developed for bicycles. The first differential drive system was developed for a bicycle, as was the first rack and pinion steering system. The museum has originals of these and many other mechanical marvels. An Irish veterinarian desiring to make his bicycle ride smoother created the first pneumatic tire for a bicycle. His name was Dunlap. In 1880-1890, the League of American Wheelmen lobbied for better roads for their high-wheel bicycles. This organization evolved into what is now the American Automobile Association. The displays of the many intricate, functioning machines, created by comrades of Wilbur and Orville Wright, show the ingenuity of the era.

We bicycled across the northern side of the Finger Lakes region. Glaciers augured these lakes to remarkable depths. Although averaging only two miles wide, Lake Seneca's depth is more than 630 feet, with 180 feet below sea level. It has been used as a testing site for U.S. submarines and submarine radar. The great depths can easily be imagined when it is time to pedal east or west up from the lakeshore. The steep grades that make these narrow lakes so deep extend out of the waters to the mountains on their sides. Immediately we are pedaling in our lowest granny gears, very slowly struggling to the top. (Granny gear is the very lowest gear and smallest chain-ring, in which we travel very slowly, but it enables steep climbs.)

The Finger Lakes consist of eleven lakes. Canandaigua, Keuka, Seneca, Cayuga, Owasco, and Skaneateles are the larger lakes. This region and its microclimate produce world-class wines. The United States government's Alcohol and Tobacco Tax and Trade Bureau designate the Finger Lakes region as an American Viticulture Area (AVA). The Cayuga Lake area and the Seneca Lake area are further classed within the Finger Lakes region as distinct AVA regions. Each of these appellations has been so designated because of the favorable microclimates and soils for growing grapes and producing wine. Most of the wineries are small operations. The distance between wineries is farther than between those in California's Napa and Sonoma Counties; thus, there is less congestion when one tours the New York wineries. Vast acres of farmlands produce crops other than grapes, such as corn, hay, wheat, oats, barley, and soybeans. Large dairy farms also fill the area. Amish homesteads offer their fresh home-baked breads for sale from their property beside the road.

The Finger Lakes region swells of early American history. Clara Barton, founder of the American Red Cross, maintained a country residence in Dansville, west of the lakes. The first local society of the American Red Cross was established there. The second and third local societies were in nearby Rochester and Syracuse, north of the lakes.

After the Civil War, Harriett Tubman made her home at the north end of Owasco Lake, in Auburn. She escaped from slavery in Dorchester County, Maryland and personally assisted more than three hundred others escape via the Underground Railroad. She was a good friend with William and Frances Seward, who also lived in Auburn. William Seward, a former New York state governor, had been a US Senator and served as Secretary of State under President Lincoln.

At the south end of the Keuka Lake is the town of Hammondsport where Glenn H. Curtiss was a bicycle racer, a Western Union bicycle messenger, and a bicycle shop owner. He is better known as the Founder of the American Aviation Industry. He did for aviation what Henry Ford did for the automobile. Curtiss met with the Wright Brothers and offered repeatedly for them to put one of his lightweight, high horsepower engines into their aircraft. The Wrights repeatedly refused his offers. Two years after the initial meeting with the Wright Brothers, Curtiss' first airplane was flying in 1908.

Curtiss accepted Dr. Alexander Graham Bell's offer in 1907 to be the Director of Experiments at the Aerial Experiment Association in Halifax, Nova Scotia. Curtiss incorporated technological innovations into the production of aircraft, leading to a long list of firsts: first aircraft equipped with wheels, first aircraft controlled by ailerons, first U.S. licensed aircraft manufacturer, first radio communication with an aircraft in flight, first takeoff and landing on water, first retractable landing gear, first successful takeoff from a U.S. Navy ship, first firearm use from aircraft, first simulated bombing from an aircraft, first aircraft sold to the U.S. Army. Curtiss won the Scientific American trophy and $2,500 prize for the first official airplane flight. He won the Joseph Pulitzer, $10,000 prize for his 152-mile flight along the Hudson River from Albany to New York City. He was the first American to win the International Air Show competition in Reims, France. Curtiss established the first flying school and trained Blanche Stuart Scott, the first female American pilot. He established the first military aviation school and trained the first two Navy pilots. Those accomplishments were before 1911. Curtiss' list of firsts continued through the years.

Car racing enthusiasts know of the track south of Seneca Lake near the town of Watkins Glen. The Mormon religion was founded in Palmyra, north of Canandaigua. In the late 1800's, the town of Corning, south of the lakes, transformed from a rail and commodities hub to the glass manufacturing giant. In 1865, Cornell University was founded at the south end of the Cayuga Lake. Today, this research powerhouse is one of the eight Ivy League schools, attracting top-tier students and faculty.

We visited the imposing Canandaigua courthouse where the trial of Susan B. Anthony was held June 17, 1873 on the charge of illegal voting. Other women had been arrested, as were the officials who had registered the women. Only Susan B. Anthony was brought to trial. The alleged crime had occurred in Rochester on November 5, 1872 during the presidential election. If Miss Anthony were to be found guilty in this criminal court, her intentions were to appeal her case to the Supreme Court to rule on the constitutional rights of women to vote in federal elections. Laws regarding voting rights were determined within each state. Her defense was the first section of the Fourteenth Amendment, which declares, "All persons born…in the United States…are citizens of the United States…No state shall make or enforce any law which shall abridge the privileges…of citizens of the United States."

The trial received tremendous attention; the courthouse was crowded with reporters and spectators. The thirteenth president, Millard Fillmore, was in attendance, as were U.S. congressmen. Susan B. Anthony was well known from her travels throughout the nation and her lectures on social improvements: temperance, anti-slavery, inequality, and women's rights. In 1872, she had traveled over 13,000 miles and spoke at 170 meetings. Susan was known at the United States Capitol and expressed her femininity by wearing a bright red shawl over her conforming black dresses. The saying in Washington, DC was that spring is no longer heralded in by the red-breasted robin, but by the red-shawl Susan speaking on the steps of the Capitol.

Judge Ward Hunt had been recently appointed by President Grant to the United States Supreme Court and was riding circuit. Until 1891, Supreme Court justices traveled the circuit via horseback to rule locally over cases. The Eastern Circuit covered Maine, Vermont, New Hampshire, Massachusetts, Rhode Island,

Connecticut, and New York. President Grant's administration had great interest in the resolution of this case and the precedent that it would establish.

The defense attorney, Henry R. Selden, called Miss Anthony to take the stand, but the US District Attorney, Richard Crowley, objected and Judge Hunt sustained that (because she was a woman), "She is not competent as a witness in her own behalf."

After Selden's argument for Anthony and Crowley's response, Judge Hunt read an opinion, which he had prepared before the trial had begun, "The right of voting, or the privilege of voting, is a right or privilege arising under the Constitution of the state, and…do not see how it could be a violation of any right derived or held under the Constitution of the United States." Judge Hunt then directed the twelve-man jury, "I have decided as a question of law…under the Fourteenth Amendment…she was not protected in a right to vote…there is no question for the jury and that the jury should be directed to find a verdict of guilty." Selden protested and requested that the jury be polled. Hunt refused and ordered the clerk to record the jury's verdict as guilty.

At sentencing, Hunt asked the usual question, "Has the prisoner anything to say why sentence should not be pronounced?"

"Yes, your honor." Anthony replied, "I have many things to say; for in your ordered verdict of guilty, you have trampled under foot every vital principle of our government…My natural rights, my civil rights, my political rights, my judicial rights, are alike ignored. Robbed of the fundamental privilege of citizenship, I am degraded from the status of a citizen to that of a subject; and not only myself individually, but all of my sex, are, by your honor's verdict, doomed to political subjection, under this, so-called, form of government."

"The court orders the prisoner to sit down." Hunt shouted, "It will not allow another word. The sentence of the court is that you pay a fine of $100 and the costs of prosecution or serve ten days in jail."

"May it please your honor," Anthony responded, "I shall never pay a dollar of your unjust penalty...And I shall earnestly and persistently continue to urge all women...Resistance to tyranny is obedience to God."

Judge Hunt then said, "Madam, the court will not order you committed until the fine is paid."

The judge's illogical and contradictory statement forced a stalemate. Hunt did not have her put in jail. Miss Anthony could not appeal Hunt's decision to the Supreme Court. Anthony had been denied a proper trial by jury. Although Miss Anthony continued her right of free speech, it was another fourteen years after her death, before the right for women to vote was secured when Congress ratified the Nineteenth Amendment in 1920.

This rural Finger Lakes region is one of the treasures of the great state of New York. The area offers its explorers excellent wines, glacial lakes, extensive wild game lands, vast farmlands, several state parks, and abundant historical areas. Treat yourself to nature and history. Take a vacation there.

Gold and Green

America by Bicycle had two large passenger vans. By their paint color, we knew them as "Gold" and "Green." Green had a diesel-driven engine and pulled a six-foot by twelve-foot enclosed trailer that carried the cyclists' and staffs' duffels and occasionally a bicycle or two. The tops of both vans were fully equipped with several sturdy, bicycle-carrying racks. Each van also had a bike rack on the rear, which was easier to get to than those on the roof. They were prepared that if weather or any unplanned event or unexpected occurrence prevented many or all of us from cycling, the vans could transport all our bikes plus all our gear and us.

Excellent Staff

America by Bicycle had three staff members on our Cross Country Challenge. Andy Hiroshima from Sacramento, California was our Tour Director. Jim Benson from Lincoln, Vermont was our mechanic. The calm demeanor, broad smile, and understanding encouragement from Christine Leininger from Coatesville, Pennsylvania was valued by all of us. Michelle Sahli from Glen Oaks, New York joined us the first week and the last two weeks of the tour, adding another encouraging, knowledgeable, and cheerful person to the staff. Each day, one of the staff had the pleasure of bicycling the route. On some days, they split the driving and cycling so that one bicycled from the start of the day's route; the other person bicycled to the end.

There were only five rest days on that central crossing, but staff did not rest even on those days. They would be washing out and disinfecting the water jugs, washing the vans, sorting the stuff inside the vans, and taking inventory of bananas and snacks. They would make a grocery store run for more of those consumables. They would be busy researching and telephoning local bike shops to determine which may have the best choice of road and touring accessories, parts, clothing, and tools, appropriate for our particular needs. Sometimes one store did not stock all the needed supplies, so two or more had to be visited. Staff had to obtain driving directions to the various shops. At the designated time, we all met to ride in the van to the bike shop. The mechanic was busy all day making adjustments and minor and major repairs to many of the bikes.

I was amazed at how quickly Jim or Andy would show up to assist with mechanical needs or to fix a flat. One day when we were cycling together, Sandi Beach had a flat. We barely began taking the tire off the bike, when Jim pulled up in the van, parked, and was taking over the task. On our first rest day in Pueblo, Utah, I had a flat on my way back from a pedicure. I was able to ride to the motel parking lot before I became aware of it going flat. I started changing the tire and was about to put the new tube in, when Jim swiftly picked up the tire and located the tiny wire that had caused the flat. I had never looked for the source of the flat, and that tiny wire surely would have given me another flat. Jim went back to servicing another bicycle on the bike stand, but Andy took over replacing the tire for me. I was grateful.

On the morning of our fortieth day, in Richmond, Indiana, I had a hotel room flat. I never realized the tire was flat until it was time to pedal away. Most everyone had already gone. The stresses of my experience on this crossing had worn me down. This was the morning after losing my tooth. Although I began going about what I needed to do to change the tire, I was moving slowly. I was nearly in tears because of the stream of difficulties that I had been encountering. Both Jim and Andy took over and relieved me of the frustration.

At the end of every day's ride, staff would set up a white board with information announcing the time of the night's meeting and where and when dinner would take place. Also, they would set out a United States map, updated each day, with the route we traveled marked in dark ink. The website for America By Bicycle is www.abbike.com.

6

Why We Ride

Why do we bicycle across the United States? There are many answers. It is an excellent way to meet the local people across the country. It broadens one's horizons by experiencing the land that others live in; seeing their homes, communities, and way of life; and by meeting and talking with those people.

For some, the answer is the same as it was for George L. Mallory, who in March 1923 answered the New York Times interview question on why he wanted to climb Mount Everest, by saying, "Because it is there."

Some people have to set a goal and prove that they can achieve it. Michelle Sahle, from Glen Oaks, New York cycled across the country to prove a point to her boss. He said that she could not do it. In 2004, in defiance, Michelle bicycled from the Pacific Ocean to the Atlantic Ocean. Her boss was wrong.

Some bicycling enthusiasts dream for years of cycling coast to coast. They truly want to pedal their bicycles every inch, from sea to shining sea. When Neil Sardiñas from King of Prussia, Pennsylvania was a teenager, he wanted to pedal across the country with some high school friends. Instead he went to college. After graduating, he longed to join college friends setting off to pedal the crossing, but Neil accepted a full-time job. Years later, he married Lydia, established a comfortable, loving home, and raised two girls. More years passed, Neil's daughters became teenagers, and Neil still had his personal dream to bicycle across the United States. After many years of establishing a healthy home and providing for his family, Neil was ready for his turn. In 2005, when he was fifty, with encouragement and support from Lydia, Neil rearranged his life and made the time so that he could pedal his bicycle every inch from the Pacific Ocean at San Francisco, California to the Atlantic Ocean at Portsmouth, New Hampshire.

A few people have pursued the crossing as a means of losing weight. That could be dangerous. Day after day physical demands on the body burn huge volumes of calories and definitely build great muscle mass. The danger is in not sustaining sufficient nutrition for the body's accelerated needs, thereby risking weakness and sickness.

Andy Hiroshima from Sacramento, California commented that some use the cross-country cycling experience as a way to escape something. Perhaps they are trying to make sense of, adjust to, or accept and overcome a loss, sadness, or tragedy in their lives. Bicycling is excellent therapy; it is a way for a person to clear his or her mind.

For some, the coast-to-coast bicycling provides a sense of freedom and independence – the American spirit. Stirred by vicariously living as the cowboys on television, whom they grew up with, the journey can satisfy that frontier spirit. It can fulfill a sense of rugged individualism. Being out there on a bicycle, powered by one's own physical capabilities, settles restlessness. Bicycles provide autonomy and mobility; things Americans love.

Shock of 9/11 – Why My First Crossing

My first experience bicycling coast-to-coast across the United States was in 2002. My friend, Susan Chapman from Frederick, Maryland, proposed that we bicycle across the country. The unbelievable horror of the World Trade Center towers coming down was the motivator. Thoughts of, "If not now, then when?" and "Why am I working so hard?" goaded me. My employer showed appreciation of the many years of engineering that I had contributed by allowing me to take time off without pay. The southern crossing route was my initiation into bicycling seven weeks, day after day, coast to coast, across the United States.

Reminiscing – Why My Second Crossing

In January 2003, I sat with several co-workers at the Ruby Tuesday's Restaurant near our office in Germantown, Maryland. It was lunchtime, but mostly we all just had several drinks. Consumption of alcohol, especially at lunchtime, was not our normal mode. We were totally unprepared when we had been told to pack our personal belongings and leave that day by noon. Our start-up company was eliminating its engineering team. We, the workers in the trench, were caught totally by surprise.

We had recently implemented and been testing physical, power-line units that were delivering high-speed Internet access to homes via the ubiquitous power line outlets. The data passed nearly error free at screaming throughput speeds of four megabits per second. Our minds had been focused on engineering: designing, implementing, and testing this exciting, leading-edge technology. We were witnessing our physical creation as it performed with very few throughput errors. Perhaps we were thinking Initial Public Offering, but definitely not layoff.

A few days later, at my home, I was catching up on my personal email. With the lay off, I now had time to do those personal things that I often neglected during my long hours at the job. I sent off an email to Jeff Schlieper, whom I had come to know while bicycling the Southern Crossing Tour. I filled him in on all the things going on in my world. His reply was, "Good for you! Now you can bicycle the American Lung Association's Big Ride." I emailed back, "Chuckle, chuckle! No, I am going back to work." However, Jeff had planted a seed. My subconscious nurtured that seed. Recalling memories of the euphoria from the previous crossing encouraged its vibrant bloom.

I recalled how physically fit I had become as a result of the crossing. My heart and lung circulation systems were at their best. Although my body has never been a lean, mean, racing machine, my muscle mass had been optimized. I was drawn to regenerating that vibrant, physical vitality.

I remembered the inspiring beauty while being immersed in nature day after day and week after week. There were memories of the sweet scents of jasmine, honeysuckle, wild roses, buttercups, and pine. I recalled inhaling the unique aromas of the dry southwest in contrast to the moist, rich soils of the Appalachians. I recalled images of the glorious colors of new blooms, whether they were the contrast of rich yellow, purple, blue, or orange surrounded by the barren southwest rock, or the acres of blazing, cheery sunflowers in the east. I envisioned acres of honey oats, the striking yellowish hue of milo sorghum, and the rich yellow of cactus flowers.

I will never forget staring into the tiny, examining, brown eyes of a round, gray, western hummingbird. I had stopped cycling and was standing awhile, admiring the cliff walls all around me. I heard the bird's wings as it zipped in from my left, and my eyes noticed its quick approach. Initially I thought it was a dragonfly, but the pitch of the sound was not that of a dragonfly. As I turned my head to see what it was, it stopped. It just hung there as I looked at it. It stared back at me as it hovered barely ten inches from my face. I stared at it in awe as it hovered there examining me.

Similarly, I can never forget the distinctive sound of the mass of swarming bees, which collectively and slowly crossed the deserted road. I clearly remember the adrenaline rush that made me leap up,

sprint away, and hope that the queen did not settle
shiny yellow bicycle.

I recollected some of the days when I felt the weather with my
entire being and reminisced of my enthusiasm at being surrounded by
nature. I remembered my hot, glistening, sun-screened skin as we
crossed the dry southwest. I recalled not being able to climb a
10,000-foot mountain pass swiftly enough to beat the approaching
lightning storm, which caught and pelted me with frozen ice pellets.

The simultaneous, intense stimulation of these senses awakened
in me a sixth sense – the exuberance of physical, mental, and spiritual
vigor and vitality. The allure of all these reminiscences put me into
action. Thus I began the process of fund raising for the American
Lung Association and made arrangements for my second coast-to-
coast bicycling adventure.

Defiance – Why My Third Crossing

In 2005, when my new employer announced that they were
shutting down the assembly line, I learned that I would be swept up
in their reduction in force. In defiance, I signed up for my third
cross-country journey. "Fine, if they are going to lay me off, I am
going to bicycle across the United States, again. I will bicycle the
central route!" I pulled out my credit card and registered for America
By Bicycle's Cross Country Challenge. Shortly afterward, I had
second thoughts about why I would want to bicycle across the
country again. It is exceedingly hard and unendingly demanding.
America by Bicycle, like most bicycle tour operators, would not give
refunds. I was not going to forfeit that money.

Then came the notion of writing about coast-to-coast bicycling.
Three crossings should give me some credibility to speak of the

experience. I do not remember how the seeds of thinking to write this book were planted; however, the thought quickly took deep roots. The book and the ride began to feed each other. If I were going to write the book, I should bike across again. If I were going to bike across again, then I should write the book.

Still I questioned why I wanted to bicycle across the country again. I had already bicycled the southern route and the northern route. I began to think of so many other things I could do with my newly acquired time. I love the nest that I call home in north central Maryland. I treasure nature's riches that abound at my country home. I could savor the fresh cut tastes of local fruits and vegetables as they ripened into their season. I could behold the beautiful colors and sweet scents of the tiger lilies, day lilies, and gladiolus that proliferate in the flowerbeds surrounding my home. I could thrill at the sights of the slim eastern hummingbirds hovering outside my window as they lavished in the nectar of those lilies and gladiolus.

Repeatedly, I questioned why I should bicycle across the country again, a third time. Yet always with those questions and apprehensions came the excitement of being out there. I was lured by the wonderful healthy condition my body would transform into. The sublime awakening of every physical sense calms the mind and exalts the soul. Memories of nature's beauty from previous journeys stirred in my consciousness.

At the root of it all, maybe I just needed to get away from keeping up on the news of the world. I had become a stick in the mud. My office mate would talk about his delicious savory deli sandwich: how he could eat one every day, and never cease to relish it. All I could think to reply was how the people in Darfur would never have such pleasure even one time in their life. The guys in the office would talk about football teams and their grandiose high-definition entertainment centers; I would think of our quagmire in Iraq. They would talk of their newborn and two-year-old children, and I would think that they should be glad they did not have teen-aged children committing to military duty. The many lives that have been altered by our actions in Iraq troubled and saddened me.

The more I tried to be a responsible citizen and get the facts, the deeper I dropped. I was hearing too much about depleted uranium, go/no-go pills, friendly fire, weapons of mass destruction, no weapons of mass destruction, exit strategy, no exit strategy. We were told that Iraqi oil would pay for reconstruction, but the multi-billion dollar budget had to be increased to pay for our operations there. We were told Iraqis welcomed the United States with open arms, but free-speech TV broadcasts aired Iraqi businessmen stating that they did not want us there. I was sick of the neo-conservatism, fear-based control warning about the terrorist threats. I kept hearing Roosevelt's words, "The only thing we have to fear is fear itself."

Meanwhile, our irresponsible and frightening lack of concern for, and detrimental actions contributing to global warming seemed to be of little concern. I did not like the role my side was playing, I could not stop thinking about it, and I could not change it. I donated to organizations trying to change things. Nothing changed. There was much more money invested in getting the big money players even more money. My donations seemed wasteful. I would go to parties, and because the issues were on my mind, I would make comments that had to remind these partygoers that people in other lands were not having such a gay old time. I needed to disconnect. This lifestyle was giving me stress and making me depressed. Two months of demanding, all-day, physical exertion pedaling from San Francisco to Maine was the medicine I needed. I made a one-way flight reservation to San Francisco and began boxing my bike.

Bob Morgan

The tenth day of cycling on the Northern Crossing, somewhere in Montana, along the miles and miles of no convenience stores, few homes, farms, or cars, I matched pace and bicycled side-by-side with Bob Morgan, Jr. from San Jose, California. We talked about many things: the weather, the sights, the tour staff, our peanut butter and jelly sandwiches, our bikes, our homes. Then in Bob's soft-spoken voice, I heard his story. He was forty-seven. He and Judy, his wife, have three children. Bob has been a cycling enthusiast nearly all his life. His cycling began with his first bike at age seven. In his teens, the bicycle allowed him to expand his world as he increased the distances he traveled. When he was twenty, he bicycled 4,200 miles across the United States in sixty days following the Bike Centennial route.

When he was forty-five, on a Sunday night in December 2000, he became nauseated and had a terribly painful headache. Through his left eye, he had a blind spot in his vision that he could not clear. He attributed the vision problem to his headache and attempted to sleep off the pain. In the morning, his face was numb. The medical professionals at the hospital informed Bob that he was having a stroke. He was immediately admitted to the hospital for appropriate medical attention and monitoring.

All I could do was stare at him in amazement. This healthy, fit guy cycling along side of me was telling me that he had just had a stroke. He was riding a nice Bianchi road bike, and he displayed the proper bicycle riding form. A stroke at forty-five! That explained why I was able to keep up with Bob's pace. We bicycled many days and many miles together.

We missed a route sheet turn on one of those days. I was out front enjoying the descent and strong tailwind. When the road flattened, Bob pulled along side me where I could hear him. He said that he thought we had missed a turn. We did. Surely however, we did not want to retrace our path up the hill and into that direct, strong headwind. I was pleased that Bob had brought an area map. We studied it and talked with a local couple, who were out on their farm for more navigational input. Eventually we found the back way into the next SAG stop to reconnect with our tour group and the route. Over the miles, I learned more about Bob's experience.

The medical experts say Bob has good collateral circulation. When the artery on the right side of his head became blocked, his brain acquired blood flow from the left side. All the bicycling he had done over the years probably helped develop this good circulation. Bob believes that it saved him. After an extended stay in the hospital, Bob was permitted to go home to convalesce. Although he still had problems with vision in his left eye, the numbness and other ailments had eased. A year later, his vision eventually cleared. Miraculously, the artery has since healed, and the blood is flowing through it again.

Bob's cycling was understandably curtailed in 2001 while he recovered. Eventually, he started riding around his neighborhood. He returned to his job, and occasionally he would bicycle to work. In late 2002 he learned that the American Lung Association's Big Ride Across America was being resurrected. Previously in 1998, he had inquired about the Big Ride. At that time, he could not be away from his family nor take seven weeks off work. His father had emphysema, and Bob had wanted to help raise funds for the Lung Association.

In 2002, Bob was still interested, and this time he would have enough vacation time saved to join the seven-week tour in 2003. Robert, Sr. was supportive. Judy, Bob's wife, was confident of Bob's abilities and encouraged him. She knew how much he loved cycling and that the exercise was beneficial for his health. Bob talked to his boss who was also supportive. Bob, however, began to worry whether he was ready for the coast-to-coast demands. For the past several years, he had been riding only occasionally. Although he started riding more in January 2003, he still was not sure he would be physically prepared for the effort, energy, and persistence that a cross-country bicycling venture requires. It was scheduled to begin in just six months.

In March 2003, Bob's world received another dramatic change. Robert, Sr. passed away. He had several health problems along with the emphysema. With this loss and sadness, Bob resolved that he would bicycle the Lung Association's Big Ride. He devoted his fund raising efforts and his intensified physical conditioning in commemoration of his father. His training now had purpose. He bicycled to and from work every day. The distance was a flat fifteen miles each way. As he shaped his body into better cycling condition, he added fifty mile rides on the weekend. By the time June arrived, he was cycling 250 miles a week.

When Bob told his neurologist of his desire to bicycle across the country, the neurologist was totally opposed. The doctor was concerned that Bob would become dehydrated, and that could cause another stroke. Bob registered the doctor's words; Bob continued training.

Additionally, Bob has type two diabetes. His endocrinologist was more supportive of the coast-to-coast bicycling venture. It was the nurse, however, whose encouragement deeply influenced Bob. She told him that situations could change in his life and that he may never have the opportunity later; thus, he should do the ride now.

A few weeks before the start of the coast-to-coast tour, Bob went back to the neurologist. Bob told him that he still wanted to do the ride. Bob assured the doctor that the ride was an organized, supported tour and that he would have plenty to drink along the way. He explained that stops for rest, water, and food are planned into each day's route. The cyclists had support vehicles with them that would also carry water, Gatorade, and snacks to replenish the cyclist's supplies along the route between stops. Bob further explained that the staff, driving the vans, follow the cyclist's progress and could transport a cyclist and the bicycle at any time that the cyclist wanted or needed. This time his doctor acknowledged Bob's determination, physical fitness, and impressive recovery. He cautioned Bob not to become dehydrated. Bob carried a 3-liter Camelbak hydration system on his back along with two water bottles on his bike.

The first day on the Big Ride was difficult. It was eighty miles with many demanding, steep foothill climbs followed by a three-hour climb into the Cascade Mountains to our overnight camp. Bob was one of the last riders into camp, but he had pedaled it all. He had pains in his knees because of all the climbing. The next morning he was strong, but after sixty-five miles, his knee began throbbing again. He sagged (i.e., he was transported in the SAG vehicle) the last ten miles. The following day, after seventy-seven miles, he again decided to sag the last ten miles. The fifth day in Spokane was a rest day when Bob's knee was not stressed and could recover. For the remainder of the tour, Bob paced himself appropriately and geared down on the climbs. Bob bicycled every inch after that from Spokane, Washington to Washington, DC. Except for the twenty-mile gap along those days between Seattle and Spokane, Bob bicycled 3,288 miles coast to coast across the United States.

John Clark

John Clark from Gales Ferry, Connecticut was motivated to bicycle across the country to raise funds and awareness to assist and support those afflicted with Alzheimer's disease. John's Mother, Vivian, was diagnosed with Alzheimer's disease for the last fourteen years of her life. Since 1999, John's bicycling promotions have raised over $94,000 to support the Alzheimer's Association. John used the coast-to-coast cycling to sound the needs of those afflicted. He met his 2005 goal of collecting $16,000 in donations for the association. John's website is www.RideForAlzheimers.com.

Our fourteenth day of cycling the Cross Country Challenge was seventy-five miles from Provo to Price, Utah. We climbed from Provo at 4,500 feet to Soldier Summit at 7,447 feet. As I began the descent down the eastern side of Soldier Summit, John was far ahead of me. Along this state Route 6, the highway was only a two-lane road with much traffic in its usual hurry. The shoulder was nearly nonexistent: very narrow with a sharp drop off from the broken edges of the blacktop to the rocks and gravel. We had a gradual descent from the peak into a strong headwind. Most of my attention was on being safe from the large volume of high-speed traffic and the narrow shoulder width.

In an instant, my front tire was flat, and I was riding on the rim. I was not traveling fast, and I was able to keep the bike in control. I stopped, took the wheel off the bike, and began removing the tire to locate the source of the flat. My front tire had picked up a piece of truck tire reinforcement wire. As I was examining the tire, there was John. We had not really been cycling together, but when John looked in his mirror for me and realized that I was no longer behind him, he pedaled back to check on me. He had been worried because of the heavy traffic and narrow shoulder and wanted to ensure that I was safe. I was impressed that he would pedal back up hill for this. Nobody ever backtracks on a long cycling trip, and especially not on a long coast-to-coast ride. Furthermore, no one backtracks up to a summit. But John did. He took over changing my tire and pumped it up to a much higher pressure than I could have.

We shared the remaining thirty miles of cycling that day. They were an exceptional thirty miles and I was glad to have shared them with John. Together we appreciated the nature around us. On one of the fast downhill sections, tucked behind the bend was a splendid twenty-foot sheet of water falling from the cliff wall. At its bottom was a perfectly shimmering, delightful pool. We hit the brakes, stopped, parked the bikes, and climbed over the guardrail. We walked across the rocks, photographed each other, and treasured the mesmerizing splash of the water into the bowl.

The scenes along the route on that day were glorious. Along the western climb there were wonderful views of farmland along the mountainsides. We had varied views of sheep, cows, and horses with crop fields filling in other sections. Isolated farmhouses affirmed the independence and self-reliance of the people who had established their American Dream there. The widespread outbuildings and fenced areas expressed the interests and priorities of their owners. The properties suggested years of hard labor and pride in their ownership.

The winding railway and the many, long freight trains traveling along our route that day added to our thrill of experiencing the nation. Seeing the trains disappear into a mountain tunnel added to the attraction. The eastern descent accentuated our impressions as the road wiggled by the base of the abrupt height of Indian Head Peak. Precipitous cliff walls towered close along both sides of us as we came through the narrow Price Canyon and into Helper.

We giggled at the intensely strong head winds blowing up into the canyon that nearly held us stationary even as the grade was descending. Thanks to John's strong cycling abilities, he was able to push through those headwinds that continuously opposed our progress on the flatlands. With me close in tow, we moved farther along and finally into Price. I am thrilled to have shared passage through that unique and special area with John Clark.

Jack Shubert and Kathryn Reid

A year before the 2005 crossing, neither Jack Shubert from Houston, Texas nor Kathryn Reid from San Diego, California owned a bicycle. Kathryn's sister, Kristina Reid from San Francisco, convinced her that the sisters should share the journey. Similarly, Steve Colburn from Houston talked Jack, his long-time friend and business associate, into the cross-country bicycling. Both Jack and Kathryn were runners and physically fit.

Steve gave Jack extensive advice on the kind of bike and auxiliary equipment he should purchase. Jack chose a Trek Postal Service 5200 performance bike. The bike store staff put his new bike on the trainer and began the process of fitting it for Jack. He got on and off as necessary for the shop staff to make the adjustments. He purchased clip-in pedals and new cycling shoes with cleats. The cleat adjustments had to be made. The saddle adjustments were made. The handlebar height and stem lengths were tweaked. Doing this process correctly required patience and time. There were a lot of mounts and dismounts on Jack's part, with decisions of what fit best so that the mechanics could spin their wrenches and make adjustments. Finally, Jack was fitted and ready.

The shop staff took his bike off the trainer stand and walked it outside for Jack to hit the highway with his new ride. Jack swung his leg over the saddle and clipped in both feet just as he had done so many times on the trainer. Then Jack and his shiny new bike fell directly over to the side. He was so new to cycling, and with all the excitement, Jack did not think of the need to pedal and roll forward to balance.

This was not the way the shop guys expected him to hit the highway. With Jack's beginning, those guys at his local bike shop might never expect that Jack would make it across California. They might find it even harder to believe that he would make it 3,850 miles across the entire country. Jack, however, takes pride in the achievement of having bicycled every inch from sea to shining sea.

Forrest Roberts

Forrest Roberts from Los Angeles, California had been employed with IBM for thirty-five years until they needed to downsize. He was offered a severance package that included retraining in any career field he desired. Forrest chose to have IBM pay him to go to the United Bicycle Institute in Oregon where he became a Certified Bicycle Technician. Forrest was our mechanic on the Southern Crossing of 2002. On most organized, supported tours, the mechanic drives one of the SAG vehicles and Tim Kneeland, the tour organizer, had expected that Forrest would drive one of the vans. Forrest, however, had accepted the mechanic responsibilities with the expectation that he would be able to bicycle the route. At the staff meeting, only three days before the start of the tour, the disparate expectations were exposed. With only three days to the start of the tour, another mechanic could not have been arranged. Tim had no other option, but to agree to try Forrest's cycling mechanic solution.

Forrest carried a fair number of tools with him at all times in his hip pack. For more major repairs, one of the support vans would bring any required shop tools. All four of the SAG vehicles had amateur radios and all staff where required to be licensed radio operators. If a bicycle were broken and needed the mechanic's assistance, they would radio one another to locate Forrest. The closest support vehicle would pick up Forrest and his bicycle and take him to the bicycle needing repair services. That happened one day while I was cycling with Forrest. Pierre pulled the red SAG van off the road ahead of us. As we talked for just a few minutes, Pierre swept up Forrest's bike and secured it to the van's bike rack. In a breeze, they were gone. All thirty cyclists and staff agreed that Forrest's mechanical ability and availability were excellent.

Keri Ricketts

Many of the cyclists on those tours were married men with school-aged children. Their wives stayed home and tended to the needs of the nest and the children. The wives handled the mail, the bills, the phone calls, the household maintenance, the emergencies, the family, and the household issues. They encouraged their adventurous, spirited, vacationing husbands who were relaxing in the freedoms and care-freeness of bicycling every day. Keri Ricketts of Eugene, Oregon, spun that stereotype around.

Keri commemorated turning thirty years old by joining the Southern Crossing Tour. Her daughter, Brianne, was five years old and her daughter, Naomi, was three years old. Her husband, Darren, stayed home with the girls, while Keri experienced the seven-week adventure of bicycling across the country. Keri's girls shared in their mother's exciting bicycle adventure when their aunt brought them to visit the tour in San Antonio and again in New Orleans. Keri's love for her daughters was evident when they were together.

Sandi Beach McLean

Sandi Beach McLean came from Toronto, Canada to take on the Cross Country Challenge. As she had already bicycled her country's Bike Canada, now she wanted to compare Canada with the United States. Also she wanted to learn some U.S. history, and this cycling tour was her premium classroom.

She traveled the Pony Express route from Sacramento, California across Nevada, Utah, Colorado, Kansas, and into St. Joseph, Missouri. A large part of the tour route followed the mid-1800's wagon-train route. She could relate to the misery, difficulties, and many long, hot, dry days that the western settlers struggled through as they crossed the prairies and Nevada Mountains in their wagons. She learned of the United States' massive mineral wealth while crossing Nevada where signs for Bureau of Land Management were everywhere.

She won the contest on July fourth for decorating her bicycle in celebration of America's independence. She experienced 1950's giddy-girl gaiety at The White Turkey Richardson's Root Beer stand, which is a family-owned and operated, excellently-maintained, 1950's outdoor, roadside drive-in at Conneaut, Ohio. She learned early American history from the New York Finger Lakes region. She toured and sampled a few delectable tastes of the Finger Lakes wineries. Her emotions of ecstasy on the last five miles of police-escorted, victorious group riding to the Atlantic Ocean will always fill her heart. This Canadian was the one with red, white, and blue flowers in her helmet.

Mel Seidman

Mel Seidman of Glen Cove, New York rode for Ben, his grand son. Mel was our oldest cyclist on the central crossing. At seventy years, Mel was motivated to pedal his bicycle from the Pacific Ocean to the Atlantic Ocean to raise funds and awareness for The Ben's Dream Foundation. Benjamin Seidman has Sanfilippo Syndrome.

On our twenty-eighth day, our route was 108 miles from Abilene to Topeka, Kansas. It was pretty country, but terribly hot and dry. The undulating hills grew some prairie grass, but were devoid of trees. Climbing in the dry heat was wiping me out. I was ready to ride in the support van just as soon as it came along. I pedaled miles and miles and miles more, but never saw it. I pressed on in exhaustion. The route sheet informed me that a convenience store and restaurant were ahead at seventy-two miles. Of course, it had to be at the top of the climb.

I dragged my exhausted body into the gravel parking lot and parked my bike in front of the building where it was blatantly visible so that my saving SAG van could see it and pull in to pick me up. I knew that the next time I moved that bike, I would be putting it onto the van. Inside, I ordered a cold drink and a sandwich; then I collapsed into a booth. The air conditioning was soothing, but my body had a tremendous amount of heat to dissipate. A wall of glass enclosed the front side of the restaurant with a relaxing view overlooking the recreational Lake Wabaunsee oasis. I was completely comfortable and relaxed there watching for the return of the SAG van.

I had been there thirty minutes, and was still exhausted from the heat, when I was surprised to see Mel and other riders pedaling into the parking lot. I had thought that they were all ahead of me, but they had missed a route sheet turn. They joined me there for their lunch. There was absolutely no place else they could have found that day for lunch. The sandwiches were good, the store's staff was pleasant, and the view was soothing.

After my comrade cyclists had their lunch break, they gathered up to continue on. I told them, "Have fun. I will see you at the motel." Mel questioned why I was not going with them. He encouraged me to join them and said that he would bicycle with me. We both rode at about the same pace. I just could not let this seventy-year-old man, who was also exhausted and worn by the heat, pedal away, while I sat there waiting for the SAG van. I gathered my helmet, gloves, and water bottles and set off with Mel.

As we climbed yet another roller coaster hill, I told Mel that we were coming to the highest hill. A communications tower ahead told me that, because they are almost always located on the highest land for their best coverage. We passed the tower, but the roller coaster climbs continued. That day I pushed myself to complete those 108 miles beyond what I had wanted for Mel, who was pushing himself on for Ben.

On our thirty-second day, we rode eighty-two miles from Chillicothe to Kirksville, Missouri. As we rolled away from Chillicothe, the terrain was covered by farmlands, and the climbs and descents were gently rolling. We were mostly on quiet back roads with very few cars or trucks, and this would be a good route to talk with another cyclist. Without the vehicle traffic, we could hear each other, and we could ride side-by-side. I enjoyed talking with Mel, and together we could exhaust a subject. He is an interested, interactive, and encouraging listener and a creative conversationalist. I linked up with him that day, and we rode many miles together. Because he seemed somewhat exhausted, I did more talking than I usually do. I came up with story after story. Mel put up with me. He did not have much choice.

Each day's route sheet informed us where the SAG stops were. We also received an elevation profile for the day's ride. That day, as the ride progressed into the searing Missouri heat, the elevation profile changed to a continuous series of long and extremely steep climbs, descents, and more climbs. Many of the climbs were thirteen percent grades! These continued all the way to the Days Inn overnight motel.

Long before the scheduled checkpoint at fifty-three miles, I was physically drained by the heat and by the climbs that we were now struggling up. All I wanted to do was make it to that SAG stop, call it quits for the day, and ride in the van to the motel thirty miles farther. Thanks to my earlier desire to have Mel to talk to, I was now cycling with Mel. Because he was riding for Ben and motivated by the pledges he had for every mile that he pedaled, Mel was not going to quit the day's scheduled cycling. I could not abandon Mel now. The ride ahead was hard for him too, and he was twenty years older. One time he had said to me, regarding my not wanting to bicycle every inch of the tour, "You will be able to return some time and ride it again. I will not be able to." I knew what he meant. Every ten years of life significantly affects our physical abilities and recovery periods.

As much as I wanted to be in that van, I thought that I had to press on with Mel. Many of the cyclists said that that day's ride was the most difficult day of the entire tour. The continual steep climbs combined with the dry Missouri heat were wickedly brutal. Our shifters would continually swing the derailleur from one extreme to the other. Each very fast down hill was so quickly followed by a slow, ultra-low, granny-gear climb up another thirteen percent grade.

I was so ready to no longer have to pedal up anoth[ ] had been alone, I would have sat on the side of the road until the SAG van came by, but I was riding with Mel. He would wait for me at the top of every climb. In my exhaustion, stress, and not wanting to be agonizing up another horrendous climb; I began sobbing. I did not want Mel to know that I was crying. I did not want to make the ride harder for him, and I wanted to press on for him and for Ben. Our route continued on those steep, unrelenting climbs in that miserable Missouri heat, and now, I too was riding for Ben. I thought of all the heartaches, tribulations, depressions, and sufferings that victims of those wretched diseases (and their families) must endure. I told myself, "I love bicycling. Pedaling up these climbs in this heat should be easy." With my tears concealed behind my dark sunglasses, I pressed on.

Mel could tell that something was bothering me. I was avoiding talking. He would ask, but I told him simply and curtly that I was okay. I could not tell him all the emotions swelling through me. I was pushing on solely driven now to be "Riding for Ben." I stopped to rest several times on several climbs. Once I pedaled into a grassy area, threw the bike down, and lay down. Mel asked whether I was okay. "Yes," I said. I was not, but I could not tell him. I said, "I just need to stretch." I went through my stretching motions as I lay there sobbing in the grass. Riding for Ben pushed me on to complete that very demanding and difficult day of cycling.

To learn more about Sanfilippo Syndrome, please explore the www.BensDream.org website. Mel's son, Stuart, and Jennifer, his daughter in law, Ben's parents, created the Web pages. They, with their son Ben, are one of the families struggling with this disease. The website is dedicated to raising funds to support research and to advance awareness.

Various Professions

During these coast-to-coast cycling adventures we live a very different life. The professions of cyclists on these rides cover the full spectrum. Skip King from Las Vegas, Nevada and Dale Crockatt from Tucson, Arizona are lawyers. Cliff Curry from Bend, Oregon is an architectural consultant. Sigmund Fidyke from Mission Viejo, California and Kevin Spivey from Mableton, Georgia are software engineers. Joan Machlis is owner and manager of "Wind Up Here" in Olympia, Washington. Jack Shubert from Houston, Texas is a CEO. Susan Chapman from Frederick, Maryland is an ombudsman for seniors. Christine Leininger is a student counselor in Philadelphia, Pennsylvania. Carolyn Fugalli from New York is a teacher whose students cheered her as she updated them on her journey with photos via her website. Bill Berendsen from Byron Center, Michigan, is a mechanical engineer working on miniaturized, military, gyroscopic systems. Susan Rutherford from Redman, Washington is a medical doctor. Burt Bodtke from Bellingham, Washington and Dick Burkey from Bremerton, Washington are retired members of the military. Dan Rowe from Boston had just completed his college studies in music. He set aside his father's continual comments to find a job for the challenge of the cross-country ride. Steven Van Jepmond from Menlo Park, California is an airline pilot. Sandi Beach McLean from Toronto, Canada is a nurse. Steve Worthy from Scottsdale, Arizona is a merchant marine. Steve Clyburn from Houston, Texas is a chemical engineer. Helen Zurek from La Habra, California is director of a medical records department. My professional experience is as an electronics engineer in start-up telecommunications companies.

7

Adversities

Our average daily bicycling distance was eighty-five miles. With the day after day, week after week of cycling, saddle sores developed in areas where we never had problems on one-week tours. Muscle pains were relieved from acetaminophen, naproxen sodium, or ibuprofen, however, until the tour was completed, our bodies never received the rest required to recover those hard-worked muscles.

We started bicycling very early every morning, but because of the long distances that we covered, the energy-sapping heat could not be avoided. The sun baked and burned our skin and dehydrated our bodies. Climbs slowed us, and if we pushed ourselves too hard, knee problems forced us off our bikes for days. Even flatlands beat us up as we pedaled in the same gear and in the same cycling position for hour after hour after hour. Headwinds slowed us, kept us out there longer, and contributed to dehydration.

In the high altitudes over the mountain ranges, cold rains sapped our energy, progress, and enthusiasm. Mornings of thick fog brought us danger, because delivery trucks could not see that we were there. Rough road surfaces pummeled our upper bodies and destroyed our momentum of spinning and rolling swiftly. Rumble strips pounded our arms and shoulders. Drainage grates menacingly lurked in the blacktop like Jaws in the ocean. Deranged drivers subjected us to their insanities.

The gypsy life of packing all our belongings into a duffel bag and pushing on to another destination was wearisome, even without the extreme physical, bicycling demands. In two month's time, each of us went through mood swings that added uniquely human, unexpected dimensions of stress between riders. There were times within the group, when living and traveling together became a strain, because of the multiple, incessant challenges.

When I signed up for my third crossing along the central route, I only remembered my exuberance, pride, best physical fitness, and elation upon finishing the previous two rides. I think that I had purposely forgotten the difficulties. There were so many more fun and thrilling things that I preferred to remember. Because I wrote some of this chapter while being on the road for my third crossing, I was better able to recall the challenges and adversities of crossing this vast United States on a bicycle.

Headwinds

I do not know where the term predominant westerly winds came from. They do not exist! On all three of my eastbound, coast-to-coast tours, we crossed the plains states biting into strong headwinds. As I write this, we are on our eighteenth day of pushing into headwinds. We did have one day with tailwinds pushing us. It was a short day – only fifty-six miles. We were able to relax at our destination and had time to do laundry. The laundry was one block from the motel. We had been on the road enough days that we all had plenty of dirty clothes. With the tailwind on this short day, we were thrilled not only to have the ease of pedaling fifty-six miles, but also to be doing laundry!

On my northern crossing, we had a challenging, continuous, fifty mph headwind for thirty-five straight miles of our route across South Dakota. Even the fast, strong cyclists could average only six to eight miles per hour into the nonstop gale. For me, it required an extreme effort to maintain five miles per hour into that unrelenting infinite blast. It was going to take seven grueling hours for me to cross that thirty-five mile distance.

A huge farm tractor came by going in my direction. I mustered energy to pick up my pace and slid in tight behind it. Immediately, the sounds of the continuous wind in my ears subsided, replaced now with the sounds of the diesel engine and the clanging implement being towed. I do not know what piece of farm machinery it was, but it was BIG! – South-Dakota-plains-size. Big! It vastly occupied the entire vehicle lane. Nah-na-nah-na-nah-nah to the wind!

The implement it was pulling was some kind of rake. The many hard, thick metal tines rose up vertically from their mounts, and then made an eighteen inch arch downward to the ground. As the tractor zipped down that South Dakota road with me closely in tow, the trailing implement would bounce. As the tines bounced into the roadway, they would throw sparks. Those sparks and farm dirt, combined with diesel soot, came right on my face and my clothes. Yet, I continued to stay behind it, enjoying the fourteen mph pull, rather than having to fight that terrible headwind. When I finally finished the day's cycling, I was filthier than usual; the tractor and tines had truly made me a dirt ball. That grime has never washed out of my tank top. As luck would have it, I had been wearing my favorite, pastel yellow top.

To handle headwinds, it helps to gear down and spin. We must stay optimistic. As my friend, Forrest, tells me, on a very hot day, the winds provide welcome, cooling relief. While a breeze feels good, headwinds can just be grueling. On a hot day, they contribute to dehydration. The best strategy is to team up with other cyclists of comparable abilities and form a paceline. A paceline is the line of several cyclists riding one behind the other in the slipstream of the cyclist in front. The ride is less strenuous for the cyclist in the back. The riders take turns being at the front of the line where they have to pedal hardest.

Some cyclists do not like to ride in a paceline. In my opinion, the cross-country journey will be far more pleasurable when cyclists can share the experience, and in the headwinds, share the paceline pulls. We do not need to ride fast, and we will be better off if we do not. We should be enjoying our cycling experience and dispel any racing mentality. We do our work fighting the wind when we are pulling the front of the line. We can relax and revel in the ease and the progress we are making when we are in the middle or back of the line. Pacelines do require all cyclists to concentrate on cycling and the other cyclists in the line. We cover the distance, make the progress, and treasure the land that we are riding in and the cyclists that we are riding with.

Cold Rain

Organized tours have to stay on schedule. Lodging and meal reservations for more than thirty cyclists and staff cannot be changed. Whatever the weather, we pedal away on our bicycles. Warm summer rains can be fun. After I am forced to be outside, pedaling in a steady, warm rain, I am more appreciative of nature. Pedaling in rain all day makes me think that flowers must rejoice on those wet days.

Rains do, however, put a damper on picture taking. Unless well protected, do not carry your camera or cell phone in the rain. Most of those electronic devices have little tolerance to moisture. To protect my electronics, I carry a "dry bag," which is sold by kayaking outfitters.

The northern and central crossings are scheduled during the warm summer months. The southern crossings are scheduled for the spring. Cool rains can be tolerated with a lightweight, breathable cycling jacket. I recommend the high-visibility bicycling jackets. They are worth the extra dollars. Just as turning on headlights on rainy days provides safety by making the car more clearly seen by other motorists, the intent of the hi-viz jacket is to provide an eye-catching alert to motorists that we are there. We pray that the motorists will see that glowing, fluorescent, chartreuse color and keep us safe.

Cold rains are an entirely different issue. These are infrequent during the warm months of the crossings. Our central crossing, however, had us climbing the Sierra Nevada Mountains of California as a cold front brought chilling rains from the Pacific Ocean. At the high elevations, snow covered the ground. The soaking rain had wrinkled our fingertips. We were shivering and unable to warm ourselves even when we took shelter in a convenience store. After fifty miles of climbing in that wet cycling experience, I joined other cyclists in the warm SAG van. Some cyclists bicycled the entire day's cold, wet journey along the Interstate-80 shoulder continually being sprayed by grit and water from eighteen-wheelers and other high-speed traffic.

On my next adventure, I would pack rain and cold-weather cycling clothes to be able to continue on the bike on those rare cold days. I would pack a thin, lightweight, polypropylene balaclava; full-finger, waterproof gloves; a waterproof jacket; rain pants; winter-weight leggings; and even booties. On my budget, nylon first-aid gloves provide the water tightness and the warming layer I need for gloves. Also, I would need some means of preventing my glasses from fogging up.

Along with the pride and victorious exuberance of finishing the day's ride in that weather, there was also the experience of being closely associated with nature. With my senses enhanced and my body invigorated with fresh air and vitality, the experience of being wrapped in the vaporizing cloud formations was a stirring, spiritual elation long remembered and treasured. The euphoria stirred inside of me – subtle and undefined.

Foggy Mornings

On day forty-six of our Southern Crossing Tour, we had started cycling very early from Orange Lake, Florida. We had ninety-five miles to pedal that day and needed an early start to beat some of the heat. As this was Florida, it would be very hot for a long part of the day. When campground staff served breakfast at 6:00 am in the indoor pavilion, all of us had our tent gear and travel duffels already packed and loaded on the truck.

We pedaled away from the Encore RV Park and proceeded east on Highway 318, a roadway that has no shoulder. The terrain is flat and the road is straight. There was a very dense fog that morning. We had turned on our blinking rear taillights. I do not believe that the taillights provided much alert, because the fog was extremely dense. We could barely see twenty-five feet ahead. We could hear the early-morning, delivery trucks approaching, but they probably could not see us. We heard many horns blaring very near us that morning. Several of us took panicked diversions to safety off the roadway. The sides of the road were mostly grass, so we were safe, even if the action caused us to fall. Fortunately, there were no hungry alligators in the area.

I believe the horn blaring was a reaction by the driver to the surprise of seeing us there. Some said the blast indicated the driver's anger at our being on his roadway. Either way, we had an invigorating, heart-pounding morning to remember. Thank goodness, we were all safe.

Shortly thereafter we bicycled on less traveled roads as the sun burned through the fog. Later that day, while we sat on the steps of a convenience store porch and ate our cooling popsicles, we commented on how those drivers must have thought that we were nuts to be out there cycling in the thick, early morning fog.

Poisonous Snakes and Alligators

Our need for a toilet often does not coincide with their availability. At the slower pace of a bicycle and on the less traveled back roads, many hours may pass before coming to an indoor toilet facility. Those times brought us closer to nature. Guys and gals alike sought relief behind trees, bushes, underpasses, drainage ditches, and parked cars.

As we came through the barren southwestern lands, I worried about poisonous snakes and scorpions piercing my fleshy, white derriere. I concluded that if I were to be so unfortunate to get fangs or a scorpion tail in my rump, I would remain calm. The venom circulates slowly, and I would not die immediately. There would be plenty of time to get back to the roadway where eventually a vehicle would come by. I could remain relaxed, flag down the motorist, explain my poisonous disaster, and sympathetically, they would immediately take me to medial facilities. I would be okay. No problem. Don't worry.

I did worry though when we came to Louisiana and alligator country. The thought of a gator biting my bottom scared me; I hydrated less. Also I did not seek such hidden, out-of-sight relief spots. I feared the gators more than I feared scaring motorists with my moonshine. Actually, there were very few motorists and they were mostly oblivious to my being there. It may sound crude, but at the time, it was another adversity handled with aplomb.

Bitter Drivers

It is dangerous out there. Do not tell my Mother. On the ninth day of our southern crossing, we bicycled seventy-five miles from

Mesa to Globe, Arizona. Jeff Schlieper from Vashon Island, Washington is an experienced cyclist. He has bicycled coast to coast many times. He certainly respects cars and trucks on the road and rides in a straight, unswerving line. While he was cycling alone into Globe, a car with four youths drove along side him. Although Jeff had said nothing to them and made no motions to provoke them, one of the passengers took a rock that they had inside the car and threw it at Jeff. It hit him and knocked him off the road and off his bike.

On our forty-sixth day, our route was ninety-two miles into Flagler Beach, Florida. Jim Porter from Tacoma, Washington, who was then seventy-one years old, was cycling the interconnecting access roads from the Palm Coast Parkway to Highway A1A South. As he pedaled on the shoulder, a car pulled along side of him. A passenger half climbed out of the window, put two hands on Jim, and pushed him off the road and onto the ground.

On the fourteenth day of our Cross Country Challenge, we ascended Soldier Summit in Utah. We had a three-mile, a two-mile, and then the long six-mile climb to the 7,447-foot summit. We crossed the summit forty-five miles from our morning start in Provo. Helen Zurek from La Habra, California; Gene Teaney from Charleston, West Virginia; Jack Shubert from Houston, Texas; Steve Clyburn, also from Houston; and Steve Worthy from Scottsdale, Arizona, were cycling in a line together up the western slope. They were the fastest cyclists and were far ahead. The vehicles travel fast along this state Route 6. Drivers had already passed the rest of us and knew that cyclists were on the highway and that they would have to move left.

Near the top, the highway shoulder becomes narrow. The edge of the blacktop was an abrupt one or two inch drop to rocks. The driver of a large box truck came dangerously close to those five cyclists. If the driver's intent was not to harm them, his intent had to be to scare them. Instinct and quick reaction times swept their actions as all of them heard and realized the dangerous closeness of that large truck. Each of them, in that instant of fear and panic, averted off the road. Thank goodness, the driver struck none of them. Going uphill, their speeds were slower, so veering off the road caused some skin abrasion, but no broken bones. The cyclists were rightfully furious. The police were unable to locate the driver.

Rough Road Surfaces and Rumble Strips

I was glad to be out of Missouri. I did not like their roads. They use a lot of tar and gravel. The recently repaired blacktop roads are uneven, rough, patched surfaces. The asphalt is not poured in neat rectangular shapes; rather, it is blobbed down and pressed out in any irregular direction. Bicycling across it was quite unpleasant.

The route on many days of the central crossing was on interstate highways, where the shoulders of the road were cut across with rumble grooves. It was absolutely too dangerous to veer into the highway to go around them; we were forced to roll over them. They beat up our hands, arms, and shoulders, and they hindered our rolling momentum. Having them on our path all day was discouraging.

I was glad to be wearing bike gloves when I had to ride on those rough road surfaces. I wrap my hands around the handlebars, but grip the bars lightly. White knuckle squeezing of the bars makes my upper body tense and transfers the jack hammering into my arms, shoulders, and back. I relax my grip and let the handlebars bounce in my hands. I can instantly grip the bars tightly whenever it is necessary. I try to not put weight on my hands by using my abdominal muscles to hold my torso, which minimizes the beating on my hands, arms, and shoulders. Also to ease the upper body stress, I lift off the saddle and putting more weight on my legs.

Grates

On the sixth day of the central crossing, from Sparks to Lovelock, Nevada, the distance was ninety-two miles. Paul Servais from Boyne City, Michigan abruptly and sadly ended his coast-to-coast journey that day. Paul is a fast cyclist. I rarely saw him, because all day long, he was way ahead of me sharing quick paceline speeds with the other fast cyclists. That day, those riders had two side-by-side pacelines traveling along a wide shoulder of Interstate-80. These cyclists were pushing for even more speed on a downhill grade.

On this particular downhill, one grate was wider than any other we ever encountered. It covered nearly all the wide shoulder from the guardrail on the right to perhaps ten inches from the continual, high-speed, interstate traffic on the left. The metal bars and gaps of the grate paralleled our direction of travel. It was wider than what any cyclist would want to attempt to jump. Additionally it was hidden in a sunken trough. The blacktop road surface fell away to it three inches below. It was ugly, evil, terrifying, and lurking. Just like Jaws – there was only one if its kind – and those cyclists were cycling in its territory. In a menacing flash, it had Paul.

The lead cyclists had been able to react and maneuver around it. The line was traveling so swiftly that they were not able to give warning of it soon enough. Paul left that bicycle-eating grate on an ambulance stretcher with broken ribs and a broken collarbone. Paul and his bike were soon on a plane flying back to Michigan. Anyone who has ever broken or bruised ribs knows that the recovery is painful and prolonged. The intense pain persists for more than four weeks. Just breathing hurts. At least Paul had invested in travel insurance. Providing that he could arrange the time, the tour company's fee would be paid to resume his crossing another year.

Railroad Tracks

At railroad tracks, it is advised to ride across in a direction perpendicular to the tracks. The concern is that the wheels could slip into the groove along the rail. It happens. When it does, the wheel is mangled. The cyclist is usually thrown and sometimes injured.

The bicycle also needs to be upright and vertical when crossing the tracks. Making the mistake of leaning to one side when crossing can put the rider on the ground in an instant, especially when the tracks are wet. I watched Kate Goetz from Buckingham, Pennsylvania as she moved out into the center of the roadway and crossed tracks perpendicularly. However, she was leaning slightly as she crossed and with the tracks still wet from the morning dew, the tires gave up their grip. She slammed onto the ground in an unexpected and injurious nanosecond. Keep in mind that the contact surface between the bike and the road is about the size of two postage stamps. A small amount of moisture could shear that contact tension.

Use caution when crossing railroad tracks. If necessary, stop until cars pass before moving into the vehicle lane to make the 90-degree, perpendicular, and upright crossing.

Ants

An adversity for my friend, Susan Chapman from Frederick,

Maryland was ants. The night that we had tented in Freeport, Texas, she laid her bike down in our camp field. She did not know that the rack bag on the back of her bike was resting on an anthill. Overnight, the ants were having a feast and celebrating their good fortune in having sugary sweets delivered to them. When the rains chased them out of the ground, they counted their blessings as they relocated their entire family, along with the eggs of their future generations, into the wondrous Sugar Shack of Susan's bag. By morning, they were comfortably settled into their sweet new home.

We packed our duffels, loaded them onto the truck, and pedaled two blocks to the restaurant for breakfast. Susan leaned her bicycle against a post and went upstairs. The two-block, bouncing ride had awakened the ant family. While Susan was at breakfast, they hustled about the family ant business. During the time that she took care of a few extra morning duties, most other cyclists had pedaled away for the day's ride. Even the SAG vehicles had gone. Susan put on her helmet and gloves, and not until she was about to pull her bike away from the post, did she see the pulsing, black ooze inside her bag.

Susan's seeing the huge cluster of ants in her bag was more repugnant than for Indiana Jones to see the snakes in the pit in the "Raiders of the Lost Ark." She took paper napkins and tried to fling out gobs of the ants. They carried eggs and hustled in every direction. As some crawled up her arms and legs, she shouted at them. Susan franticly jumped to shake them off, stomped on one here, jumped, and stomped on one there, as she screamed at the sensations of them crawling on her.

Now I can say that it was funny to watch her antics, but Susan saw no humor in it. Finally, she obtained Raid from the restaurant staff and settled who was boss of that rack bag. Susan still shudders at the thought of that black and white-spotted, creepy, crawly glob. She says from now on, she will have only Cliff Bloks, and no more oozing, sugary sweets.

Long Distances

It is interesting how coast-to-coast cyclists become accustomed to demanding days of eighty-five miles. When the next day's route sheet informs them that the distance is less than sixty-five miles, they refer to it as a "short day." They may start that day's ride later or have more time in camp at the end of the ride. Some may even linger longer at a town or at one of the sights along the planned route.

Our adventure is to bicycle across the United States and we have limited time to cover the long distance. Some people tell me that they would want to explore other areas. Doing so would require more time away from home and work, and more money to pay for lodging, food, and touring. The tour organizer's purpose with these cross-country journeys is to orchestrate the group across the country in the allotted time. Obtaining seven consecutive weeks free from work is the first challenge for most cross-country cyclists. There is so much to see and experience in this nation. I believe it is impossible for anyone to observe all its splendors. There is plenty to experience and remember along whichever route is taken.

My Personal Challenge

My third crossing made me realize and accept a personal adversity that I had never accepted previously. From my years as a recumbent cyclist, I had the methods of spinning pretty well at my command. On the flats and gentle grades, I could be reasonably quick. I could do a fair job when it came my time to pull a paceline, although opinions varied whether that low recumbent out front provided enough slipstream advantage to the second cyclist on an upright bicycle. However, when the grades increased even slightly, I slid off the paceline jiffy quick and was plodding up the climb alone.

That was understandable when I rode the recumbent, but when I made the transition to the conventional, upright bicycle, it was still happening. It seemed that everyone passed me. For seven years previously, I had been riding recumbent bikes. I concluded that I just had not been riding upright bikes long enough to develop my climbing legs. I heeded and incorporated all the advice I heard. My athletic body is very muscular. "You have large bones" I was told when I was a kid. My friend, Jeff Bartlett from Silver City, New Mexico calls me "Stallion Legs." Although I have this very healthy and athletic-looking body, after two years of riding upright bikes, I still could not keep up with my level of cyclists when the road grade began going up.

When the Cross Country Challenge Tour left the bay lands of California and immediately climbed the San Francisco peninsula, I was again riding solo. The continual climbing designed into this "Challenge" ride gave me many more miles of solo riding. During those times I contemplated, and finally accepted, why I could not maintain a quick pace on the up grades.

I am fortunate to have excellent health. Years ago, I arranged having annual physicals to have a baseline of my medical condition. If I ever did have health problems, I wanted to be a known patient of a good physician. My blood work always came up good. The EKG was good, but when he listened with the stethoscope, even the doctor seemed to be surprised that he was hearing a murmur. I always dismissed it. He said it was slight. My doctor assured me I was okay and that I should keep doing what I was doing. So I did.

The Cross Country Challenge finally made me understand why I could not keep up with my peers when the grades ascended. I was like a good car engine that needed a valve job and lost compression when power was needed. Instead of my heart valve snapping tightly closed, under pressure, it fluttered and let the blood leak by – thus the murmur. Finally I understood why I could not keep up the pace on the climbs. This is my little challenge I have to deal with. I can still do these rides, although at a more sluggish pace when the road goes up.

To climb the 11,312-foot Monarch Pass in the Colorado Rockies, I repeatedly bicycled five minutes and then paused for forty-five seconds to let my racing heart calm down. Keeping the pause short prevented my muscles from tightening. It took a long time to climb those Rocky Mountains, but I pedaled up them. I do not have to be fast to delight in the scenery and appreciate the distance I can cover on those two quiet wheels.

Heat

I have difficulty dealing with dry heat. In the humid Mid-Atlantic weather, where my home is located, I usually do not have problems. Moving through the humid air at bicycling speed seems to provide an evaporative effect that my body can deal with. However, in the dry heat of the southwest, high deserts, or central plains, I struggle. Perhaps the difference is not the humidity; rather, temperatures out west are higher than what I am acclimated to.

I seemed to be more susceptible to heat exhaustion than other cyclists. To lower my body temperature, I poured water on my head wherever I could find it. My friend, Forrest Roberts from Los Angeles, waited for me several times while I sought water to lower my body temperature. In the high desert plains of Washington, a rare trickling creek working its way through the scrub grass provided the cooling relief. I worried of slithering things in the grasses and under the rocks, but made lots of noise, whacked the grasses before I stepped ahead, and pressed on to the healing water.

Another time, Forrest waited while I climbed through fence wire to reach a six-foot round, two-foot high water barrel for cattle. If Forrest had not been there, I may have just gone for a swim in that little tank. With Forrest there, I tried to maintain some part of my grace and femininity and merely stepped one leg at a time up to my knee into the tank. I wear Shimano cycling sandals when I bike, with no socks, so I could put my whole foot and shoe into the water. Next I soaked my bandana and splashed my head with water. After letting

the sopping wet bandana drench my neck and torso a few times, I dipped it again, wrapped the soaking cloth over my head, tied it at the back of my neck, and put my helmet over it. I was refreshed and ready for another twenty miles until my bandanas and I evaporated dry again. Perhaps our bodies can handle dry heat better after they have a period of acclimation. Other cyclists did not seem to have problems with the heat as I did.

In the Sun All Day

Kevin Spivey from Mableton, Georgia is my hero! He was so quiet. It seemed he rarely spoke and when he did his voice was so soft. I had to really strain and tune in to hear him. Kevin has issues with the sun. He was literally covered from head to toe. He wore black socks, full shoes, bloomer-like blue or black pants, a long-sleeve yellow or white shirt, full-finger gloves, and a skullcap with neck cover. The only part of his skin that was not covered with clothing was his face, which he covered with thick, white, sunscreen protection. He was a contrast to me in my cycling sandals, no socks, bike shorts, and tank tops.

Some people whose skin cannot tolerate the sun's rays would say that they could never do a bicycle tour because they cannot be in the sun. Not Kevin! He is my hero. His skin cannot tolerate the sun, yet he was in the sun every day bicycling across the country. Kevin did not let the sun deny him of that memorable experience and triumphant accomplishment.

Knee Injuries

Climbs are never easy. Thanks to the technical marvel of gearing on our bikes, we can surmount the ascents without damaging our knees. If a car can travel a blacktop road, we should be capable of pedaling our bikes on it. I recommend that your bicycle have a triple chain-ring set. That ultra-low "granny" gear will ease the climbs and perhaps spare you from serious knee injury. If you have knee problems, let the SAG vehicle take you and your bike to the top. The solution to minimizing knee pain may be as simple as gearing down, lowering or raising your seat, or adjusting your cleats. Until you resolve how to minimize or eliminate the pain, do not stress your knees or risk tearing tissues.

Monotonous Flatlands

In crossing this country, I have found that there are few places that are really flat; however, we call them flatlands because the grades are slight. In comparison with the mountain climbs, they seem flat. Until one has had hours and days of flatlands, one may not realize how they could be an adversity. Continuously pedaling in the same gear, using the same muscles, and riding in the same position challenge the body. The constant effort, speed, and terrain can be mentally monotonous.

Headwinds, as are often encountered in those monotonously flat areas, exacerbate the flatlands challenge. I had to learn to pedal standing up to give my body a change. Usually, I have to gear up two increments; then I stand up and pedal. I try to pedal fifteen to twenty-five revolutions while standing. When I sit down again, my pelvis will be in a different place on the saddle, which provides some relief for the buttocks. By standing, my speed increases, which helps maintain a quick spinning pace when I settle back into the saddle.

Sometimes on flatlands I will take my cycling gloves off. I always carry them with me on the bike, ready to put back on when I need them. Unless the road surface is very rough, I like to ride without wearing them. This helps me to concentrate on using my abdominal muscles to hold my torso so that I am not putting weight on my hands. I do not recommend doing this on a very hot day when there is a concern of your sweaty hands slipping on the bars, levers, or brakes when you need the grip. On rough road surfaces I need to wear them to keep control of the bike and to absorb the pounding of the road surface. I also wear them on climbs when I need to pull up on the handlebars as I demand more from my body. When I can, however, I take them off to avoid an abrupt tan line at my wrists. Minimizing tan lines may be vain, but is desirable to me.

Gypsy Life

The gypsy life we live on these coast-to-coast rides is another nonstop, day after day, week after week challenge. Every day we must pack all our belongings and move on. Most likely we will never be back, and we must be sure not to leave any of our things behind. There is no settling, resting, or nesting. The gypsy life is multiplied over the two-month period by the changing moods of thirty-five people coexisting day and night and each enduring the multiple physical stresses. The demands may weaken the bicyclist and make one susceptible to colds or flu viruses. Paul Appert from Albany, California had to end his tour prematurely when he was overcome by a rare strain of pneumonia.

These cross-country rides can sap our energy. We must try to eat lots of healthful food, be wary of foods or drinks that harbor harmful bacteria, and avoid foods that do not smell or taste wholesome. To stay hydrated, we drink Gatorade or PowerAde and should avoid alcohol or caffeine in excess. We need to sleep restfully and keep ourselves strong to avoid a cold or flu.

Muscle Pain

Although I had intentions to be optimally physically fit and have my body toned to bicycling perfection before I showed up at the beginning of each of the three coast-to-coast tours, it never happened. Somehow, the demands of daily life kept me from obtaining the cycling time I thought I should have had before beginning a coast-to-coast bicycling journey. Thanks to modern medications, I was able to ride the days and weeks while my body and muscles were forced into cycling shape.

I remember waking up achy and stiff. I did not want to get on that bike. However, everybody was gathering up to go, and I knew that I also had to go. I would pop two, eight-hour, 650mg Tylenol before getting out of my sleeping bag. They would have time to infiltrate my blood stream while I packed my sleeping bag, air mattress, and tent. I would pop two Bufferin after breakfast, just before getting on the bike. An hour or so into the ride, my body would loosen up and the pains were gone, or at least I could not feel them. To be on the safe side and to endure, I would pop two more acetaminophen before lunch. Fortunately, my liver survived the inundation.

I do not risk generic brands to alleviate the pains. I want assurance that the drugs will assimilate into my blood stream and have the optimized pain-relieving ingredient. This is not the time for me to be saving pennies. I am worth the best meds when I am pedaling across the country. Some of the other coast-to-coast cyclists may call me a hypochondriac. Some need no pain relievers. On my third crossing, I switched from Tylenol to Motrin. As I strengthened along the journey, I discovered that I needed only two Motrin in the morning after I started cycling.

After many weeks and with my improved cycling fitness, my muscles would still burn, even on gentle climbs. Fatigued muscles never fully recover with only one rest day. My body needed a week to recover; however, my weary muscles would not have that respite until the coast-to-coast journey was completed many weeks later. These cross-country tours give me empathy with the tribulations of the Tour de France racers. Those cyclists are pushing constantly while they are on their bikes. They are racing up steep, high-elevation mountains day after day. Their leg muscles absolutely burn even more than mine and they too do not obtain enough rest to recover their muscles for the next demanding day of cycling.

At night, I knew that I needed sleep to rest my body and my muscles. I did not want to be tossing and turning or otherwise disturbing the recuperative, restful hours that my body needed. Some folks take Tylenol PM. Some take Benedryl, Sleepeaze, or Ambien. On my first coast-to-coast tour, I had taken Benedryl. It did enable me to keep my body still through the night allowing the muscles to rest and recover. However, I was groggy for a few hours into the next day, and I did not like that part. Now I prefer the milder, natural sleep-aides, such as, Calm Magnesium or Valerian Root. Although by the end of my last crossing, I must have adapted my body to the required routine as I no longer needed any of the sleep aids. It probably helped that on that third crossing we were not tenting. Snuggling into the fresh sheets of a spacious bed in a quiet motel was enough for me to rest still through the night. The hot baths probably also helped.

Susan Chapman from Frederick, Maryland is an inspiration to me when I think that my muscles ache. She bicycled across the country with Fibromyalgia inflicting her with widespread musculoskeletal pain. This chronic condition strikes throughout all the muscles; tendons; ligaments; and soft, fibrous tissues of her body. You may be able to relate by the pains you felt in your body and muscles while a bad flu sapped your energy. Susan pushed on through the shooting and stabbing pains and endured the deep muscular aching, throbbing, and stiffness. She ascended the mountains and bicycled every day across the country for 3,200 miles. Susan does not think of bicycling as exercise. For her, it is relaxing and therapeutic. She says, "Bicycling is a joy."

Saddle Sores

Cycling across the United States brings a unique significance to the term, "Pain in the butt!" High quality cycling shorts are worth their price when wearing them for eight hours or more every day. I have learned that a variety of brands are best.

I dream about bicycling…a lot. One night, in my dream, I was in a bike shop telling the sales staff how padded bike shorts just do not provide relief for casual cyclists. Unlike racers, as I dreamed the slender sales staff were, I said recreational cyclists sit on the saddle more often and for longer periods. Racers, I explained in my dream, use the seat location more for establishing their body position to the bike frame. They would mostly be powering the pedals through their legs almost as though they were running, in contrast with casual or touring cyclists, who actually sit on the seat. Thus in my dream, I told them that the bike shorts they were selling needed more padding. They needed very big, puffy pillows.

This dream must have been an omen of my experiences to come. In my awakened world of cycling, there is never adequate padding, even in the best of those shorts. Cycling eighty-five miles a day, every day, week after week, is vastly different than a two-day weekend ride or even a weeklong, bicycling, travel adventure.

On my first crossing, I rode a recumbent, so saddle sores were not a concern. On my second crossing, I rode a conventional road bike. I had several pairs of Primal Wear bicycle shorts, which I liked because the leg length was shorter and I could acquire more of a golden tan on my legs. Each pair had a different colorful side panel so I could be fashionable. I brought six pairs of them, which is more than I now recommend bringing. Because each pair was the same brand and cut and each had the same shape of padding insert, every day my legs rubbed against the pads in the same location. The continuous chafing resulted in wicked, raw skin in the groin and gluteal fold areas.

My solution was experimenting with many chamois creams and general skin creams. I put a lot of money into this experiment. I heard lots of advice. Because I had already created a problem, the creams I recommend today were not helping me through each day's ride. I went to the petroleum jelly solution. Yuck! I totally frown on the solution today, but it helped me through that crossing. Petroleum jelly does not wash out. It just spread around to all the other clothes in the washing machine with it, and all the clothes came out grimy and dingy. The other embarrassing thing about petroleum jelly is that everyone could tell where I had been sitting. Perhaps a good thing about this feature is that my saddle has become rain proof. Petroleum jelly does not offer antibacterial protection like the newer chamois creams. This protection is beneficial where in-grown hairs or chafing has occurred.

One of our riders had a boil develop in his groin area, yet he continued to bicycle. Finally, in Helena, Montana he had it lanced in the emergency room. He said that it had grown to the size of an egg. That forced him to ride in the support vehicle for a few days while he nursed and dressed the inflammation.

For my third crossing, I splurged and bought better bicycle

shorts. Previously I had been buying shorts on sale for $30 a pair. This time I splurged and bought a pair of Canari shorts and a pair of Pearl Izumi shorts that each retail for $80. For chamois cream, I had been using only Original Udder Balm moisturizing cream. It seemed to provide adequate protection during my local, weekend rides. This combination let me down with the long cycling on the coast-to-coast tour. The Udder Balm cream began to feel like an adhesive paste. On the hot days that we were cycling, the cream made the padding of the cycling shorts stick to me so there was absolutely no air circulation.

I upgraded to creams specifically designed for cycling chamois. I bought Chamois Butt'r or Assos whenever I found a bike shop that had it. When I lamented my issues to the tour director and that I had upgraded from the $30 shorts to the $80 shorts, he calmly informed me that his shorts had cost $120 and that he paid $180 for the shorts he wore the day before. Gulp! These trips usually demand unexpected expenses.

The next rest day, in Salt Lake City, I joined other cyclists in the van going to the bike shop for better long-distance cycling shorts. I found a pair of Sugoi RS Flex shorts for $110 that I now love. The chamois pad is thick, but also provides some air circulation. They have a triple layer of padding for the pelvis bone. Now when I put other shorts on, my rump misses that extra padding for my bones.

Some folks do coast-to-coast rides and never have to deal with these issues. I do not know what the secret or difference is. Alice McIntyre of Modesto, California bicycled across the country wearing shorts that belonged to her husband. I do not think she had any saddle problems. Neil Sardiñas from King of Prussia, Pennsylvania cycled across the country wearing shorts that were worn so thin that his skin showed through. He cleverly wore black underwear so that only black showed through the thinned spandex material.

I look at the pads in my $30 shorts now and wonder how I ever could have bicycled eighty-five miles wearing them. I now love my

$110 cycling shorts, but I am disappointed that the spandex material has thinned. I followed Neil's lead and tried wearing a pair of black underwear to conceal the thinning threads of my favorite Sugoi shorts. That solution did not work for me. Even though they were quality ExOfficio brand underwear, the cloth material blocked the comfort of the Sugoi pad and the seams were noticeable and uncomfortable.

My next budget solution was to wear two pairs of bike shorts. That was okay. I had the comfy Sugoi pad next to my skin. The outer pair of bike shorts provided just a bit more padding. The outer pair had a designer side panel that made my fashion statement. The dual combination provided more muscle support for my legs, and the two pairs together were comfortable. They were not too hot, but the temperatures were only in the high 80's, and I was not wearing them day after day, week after week.

When I set out on another cross-country cycling tour, perhaps I will break down and buy new quality cycling shorts. Recently, I saw a pair of Louis Garneau shorts with the new Ultra Ventilated Airstream chamois. The women's sized padding insert looked very comfortable and thickly padded. Their advertisements claim that the "fused big vents molded into the chamois quickly eliminate heat, moisture, and rainwater that cause irritation." They further claim that it is "highly breathable, hypoallergenic, and antibacterial to avoid infection and chafing." I could see what they mean by their statements of "variable thickness, flex lines and ergonomic linear channels in line with the large vents to wick moisture and heat quickly." They claim it to be the "world's most advanced, most high-tech, patented chamois." I guess it would take another analytical geek who has bicycled across the country to understand my excitement for these shorts. The $180 price tag has left me only drooling over possibly owning a pair of them. Perhaps when I sign up for another coast-to-coast tour, I can justify that very high price and treat myself.

As for chamois cream, Assos is an excellent cream. It includes an antibacterial ingredient. It works very well for relief in the groin and gluteal fold areas. Women should avoid using this product in the female area, because some of the ingredients can cause a burning sensation. I use Chamois Butt'r brand to avoid the burning, but use Assos brand for the other areas. To alleviate chafing irritations from the edge of the padding insert, I put a bead of chamois cream right on that padding edge transition. I reapply every twenty to forty miles.

After showering each day, I apply Neosporin triple antibiotic. I recommend buying and bringing a case of Neosporin on your cross-country ride. What you do not use, you could auction off among your co-cyclists. The profit you make could be a hefty contribution to a charity. Some cyclists tell me that they use Noxzema. Some say Desitin pampers their bums. I have not tried either of those. Weeklong rides do not usually create such saddle sore problems. On a cross-country ride I do not want to risk experimenting.

I recommend a good saddle. Mine is a Terry Butterfly with the cut out in the middle. Each of my bicycles is fitted with a Terry Butterfly saddle. I have seen a few bicycles with a good lightweight, women's Trek saddle, which has good sit-bone cushioning and a center cutout. However, I have not found bike shops that stock that Trek saddle for purchase.

There are other ways to prevent saddle sores. You could relocate the pressure on your pelvis by shifting around on the saddle. Put your weight on both pedals and lift off the saddle. To do this, put the pedals in the horizontal position, at the 3:00 and 9:00 positions. You could simply lift off the saddle and grip the saddle between your thighs. I recommend learning to pedal standing up. You usually need to shift up a gear or two and then stand. Count the number of pedal rotations and try to do at least ten rotations. This uses other muscle groups in your legs. When you settle back into the saddle you will be repositioned on different pressure points.

I do not have all the answers to the seat issues, although I have learned a lot more with each crossing. Only another crossing will give me more solutions. I think I would have issues then too, but perhaps now I know better how to minimize the problems. Maybe like the racers that I dreamed about, I would use the saddle just to hold my position and press and stand on the pedals as if I were running. Maybe, I would do that nearly the entire way across the country. Nah! That will not be happening; for me, that will always be a dream.

Overcoming Adversities

Although we rejoice in our cycling experiences, we must be vigilant and persistent to overcome the adversities of the road. Climbs, rumble strips, cars and trucks too close, rough road surfaces, long distances, headwinds, cold weather, dangerous bicycle-eating grates, sharp-edged holes, railroad tracks, tire-flattening glass, retread tire wires, and bitter drivers are all surmounted in our desire to cycle from sea to shining sea across the United States.

I am repeatedly impressed by the determination and persistence of cyclists. They have set their goal to ride their bicycles from coast to coast across the United States. These people are determined and surmount unrelenting adversities to achieve their goal. In the end, perhaps they also choose to remember primarily the jubilation and the fun parts of the achievement. Perhaps it is the difficulties, obstacles, setbacks, and challenges, which we overcome that make us more vigorous and vital, and lead us to an awe of creation and an appreciation of nature and its beauty.

8

The Joys

Bicycling coast to coast with an organized tour company allows our minds to be free. We connect with, delight in, and harmoniously integrate into nature. The crossing transitions our bodies into excellent shape. The experience broadens our minds and ignites our spirits. As the journey awakens all our senses, we experience the utmost vigor and vitality – not only physically, but also mentally and spiritually. We attain an incomparable appreciation for the vastness and variety of this rich nation, which is a large part of why bicycling across it is so special. We learn United States history and vicariously experience the lives of those who made that history. From college students to baby boomers to the seventy-something's, we are inspired by others, whom we ride with. Sharing the journey heightens and extends the accomplishment.

Our Minds Are Free

As they do all the support work, the tour company makes the crossing a vacation for us. We are removed from having to plan and schedule the day, the week, the next week, and the many weeks after that. We eat, we sleep, and we ride wherever the tour company tells us. It is not a dream, but a true removal from our stress-filled, day-to-day lives; it is a real vacation. These crossings become fifty consecutive days for grown-ups to be young at heart, go out, and play.

We do not need to think about what, when, or where we will eat. The menu planning of what meats, produce, dairy, or other staples to buy is not our concern. The chores of looking through the aisles for those things on our grocery list, transporting them home, unloading, preparing, cooking, and cleaning afterward are eliminated.

We do not have to handle money. In the restaurants, when we are finished, we simply stand up and walk out. We are not concerned about receiving the check or what amount to tip the servers. The tour staff handles that. We simply walk away.

The tour organization makes the reservations for where we will sleep. They have the burden of locating addresses and phone numbers for those lodgings. If we were not traveling with a tour company, we would have to scour maps to decide whether a motel or campground location would fit in with our cross-country route. We would have to make those many phone calls coordinating each overnight place for each date and negotiate that the fees are within budget.

When we travel with a tour company, they are tasked with seeking an alternate when some convention, fair, or rodeo is gathering in the town, where we thought we would spend the night, but learn that all the lodgings have already been taken. As we travel, the tour staff has the responsibility of keeping track of the contact information for each of the chosen lodgings. While we are bicycling, the staff makes phone calls reconfirming reservations a few days before our arrival. It is the tour company's concern to ensure that there are adequate food facilities within budget and within walking distance of each lodging place.

Our routine is simple: wake every day, put all our things back into our bag, and heave it onto the truck. We get breakfast wherever we are told to. Then we pedal away on our bicycles. We do not have to spend time studying maps to determine which roads we should travel, how that route will take us to the day's end, how that distance will fit in with reaching tomorrow's end, or the day after that. The tour company does the research to determine a safe route through a busy city to and from the overnight lodging. We turn left or right where the daily route sheet tells us. Keeping track of paper work does not concern us. The tour staff has the responsibility of carrying enough copies of each daily guide. Each day we receive a fresh, non-crumpled copy of the next day's route.

We do not even need to know what keeps our bicycles operating well. Whenever we hear a noise or something does not seem correct, we take it to the tour mechanic, and it is fixed. It is like being a kid. All we do is go outside and ride our bicycles all day, every day, for seven weeks. The day-to-day stress of normal life melts away and can be forgotten.

Wrapped in Nature

I experience so much life while I am cycling. Sometimes a bird will fly along parallel with me. As it swoops and rises on the wind it pushes under its wings, my spirits lift in the ecstasy of being there with it. The groaning sounds of two trees pushing against each other, as the wind brings them into animation, speak to me of my freedom to uproot and explore new areas. The mesmerizing movements of the grains, as the wind sweeps and swirls them in sinuously flowing, fluctuating waves, stir lightness into my being and open my perceptions. The dust devil, dancing left and right and forward and back, with its patter as it sweeps closer, seems to be enticing me to come dance with it. I close my eyes, as that lively devil crosses over and around me and dusts my sweaty, sun-screened body with grit. After it passes, I giggle from having been swept by the dancing devil.

We flow into the fragrances of the rose bushes along the fence.

The damp, earthy, pine-infused redolence of the Pacific Northwest seems to permeate into our blood. Thick, salt air along the coast seems to cleanse and heal even our mental and emotional wounds. The sweet scents of honeysuckle lighten our heads. The subtle whiffs of rock and tumbleweed in the dry southwest air, accentuate our 360-degree views of vast, rugged, unpopulated, colorful, and glorious earth.

Easier Than Walking

A great benefit of bicycling is that with very little physical exertion, we can roll. Even when our cycling is slow, we are making progress toward our destination. I can bicycle one hundred miles just about any day. I think it is easier than running or long-distance walking. Many of my friends have taken on the challenge of walking twenty miles a day with the 3-Day Walk benefiting the Susan G. Komen Breast Cancer Foundation. With walking, if I do not pick up that foot and press on, through blisters, or foot, ankle, knee, or leg pains of the previous day's endeavors, I will not make progress toward the current day's goal. On my bike, I press that pedal a little and roll a lot.

Another benefit of bicycling compared with walking is that I am not pestered with bugs biting my skin and sucking my blood. There is none of that pesky buzzing around my head or bugs darting into my eyes. There is no slapping my arm or neck or leg in reaction to a pest chomping into me.

Climbs, however, are when cyclists really workout, and ascents are my challenge. To me, climbing on a bike is like running. If I do not press that pedal another revolution, I am not going to make progress to the top. I try to welcome climbs and the variety that they bring. That is when my body does its exercise.

Bicycling makes us aware of distance. When a cyclist gives directions, a mile is close to being exactly a mile. Non-cyclists have given me directions, saying that the road to turn on, was two miles ahead, but instead, was five miles farther. That is a big  difference when traveling on a bicycle. Bicyclists are aware of uphill, downhill, and percent grades. One of my favorite roadway signs is the yellow diamond showing a box truck on the down side of the triangular ramp. These signs tell of descents ahead and miles of easy cycling.

A cross-country tour makes a bicyclist very proficient at following route sheet directions. A few missed turns, which make us have to backtrack and add "Bonus Miles" to an already long day, teach us to watch for all road markings. We learn that route sheet mileage is often not accurate, and we learn to accept it and deal with it. We must be vigilant for the name at each side road for a match to the name on the directions. This task is made more challenging when names do not match exactly, such as, the route sheet name is "Whispering Meadow Road," but the name on the sign is "Meadow Road."

Cyclists far ahead of us may not even be with our group, and by following wherever they go, we could quickly tack on lots of Bonus Miles. We learn to verify that the cyclist in front follows the directions correctly. Staying on route is the job of all cyclists. We each have to read the route sheet information, note our mileage, and watch for street signs. After completing a cross-country tour, the bicyclist's ability to follow cue sheets and stay on course for local club rides, centuries, or weeklong tours will become second nature.

Out of the Box

In a car, I see the country, but do not feel it, taste it, smell it, or hear it. I do not truly experience it; I am not intertwined in it. In a car, I am barreling through time and space in a contained, wheeled box. Interstate highways are excellent for shortest time to a destination, but the excitement is in the company I travel with and my expected destination. Sitting in that same static position while being perpetually inundated with mostly homogeneous sensory stimulation can make for a long journey. The monotonous frequencies of the engine and drive train and tires on the pavement are dulling and mind numbing. There is neither variation nor vitality as there is in nature. On a bicycle, I experience life at a slower pace. The quiet with no motors and no radios frees my mind to explore its own channels.

Traveling on a bicycle, wrapped in nature, with the continual productive movement of my body intensifies the senses. My smooth forward movement, spontaneous sense of balance, and being outdoors, with no limiting confines, elicit a marvelous sense of freedom and adventure. The use of my own physical power is intrinsically rewarding. Whether it is by stimulating endorphins, serotonin, tryptophan, alpha waves, or whatever mechanism, the physical exertion greatly contributes to my mental, emotional, and spiritual well-being.

On a bicycle, I am much more aware of what is happening in nature. As I cycled through a forest once, I heard an isolated rain shower pounding on the canopy of the leaves above me. Through some of the clearings I could see the thick shower of raindrops, yet I never felt a drop on me. If I had been in a car, I would not have known that it was raining directly above me.

By traveling at the slower pace of a bicycle, the scenes linger longer. The sights, sounds, smells, tastes, and touch of life are embedded deeper than they are while being in a car. There is increased sensory input, more data points, more attributes to register and associate with each of the senses, and more to put into my memories. As I view a farm with its pond, barns, and farmhouse, I have time to absorb the shapes, colors, and angles. I can study the details of the shutters, window treatments, varieties of doors, the architectural details, the shrubs, and the landscape around the house.

I envision sitting on the bench beside their pond, watching the tiny ripples at the water's edge, and admiring the skater bugs skimming on the water's surface. I imagine tasting a blade of grass in my mouth. I smell the mixture of the nearby colorful flowers and hear the whistles, chirps, and songs of the warblers, cardinals, and thrushes from the trees above and the bushes behind. The cows inside the barn, and the grain elevator feeding the silo, are not just a blurry snapshot scene, but instead are part of my vital, active day. I breathe the air, smell the grain, and hear the moos. I can almost feel the sensations on the ducks' feet as they skid on the water and land into the pond.

By traveling on a bicycle, I can stop at most any place that inspires me. I can stop any place I want on twisty, mountain roads to behold the vistas. Once I stopped along a guardrail by a lake to watch schools of glistening fish changing from one direction to another. A car would not have been permitted to stop there. While there, other fish also entertained me as they leaped out of the water for their morsels.

Because of the many days that I have traveled by bicycle, now even the car rides yield much more appreciation of and association with nature. Upon seeing clouds form and tumble down the mountain ridges, the sight stirs memories of being wrapped in similar mountain mist. I am more likely to notice hawks perched or soaring above as they keenly watch for small movements below. I admire the distinctions of color of the feathers on their breasts, wing tips, tail, and heads. Often while traveling in a car and seeing wonderful views, I want to come back and ride that area on the bike so that I can truly behold and experience it.

Pleasures of Nature

Being outside, along with the physical stimulus of cycling, heightens my awareness. I more clearly hear the songs of the birds chirping about the seeds that they have found. I delight in watching them as they chomp, cheer, and alertly watch any movements near to them. I do not need to see them, but know they are there by the sound of their wings pushing against the air. The trickling of the water down rocks in a creek that I am pedaling beside sooths my soul. The bass of the wind blowing in the trees adds to nature's symphony. Would that be called the woodwinds?

As I biked along, I had time to watch flocks of birds as they altered flight from one direction to another and back again. The sunlight reflected off the tops of their wings, and I was intrigued by their flight. I watched the glistening from the top of their wings, then the flock turns, and the glistening transitions to the flat black of the bottoms of their wings. Another turn delivers another transition to shimmering wings in flight. The entire flock simultaneously turns in formation. How do they all know which way to turn?

Even the turkey vulture with its fleshy red, ugly head becomes a beautiful creature as I watch its large wingspan and graceful soaring. My spirit lifts in association with its beautiful and effortless flight.

One time a flock of geese was flying low, close above me, and in the same direction as the road that I was bicycling. We usually just see the V-shaped flock of them and hear them. We probably do not think of the efforts they must exert to keep in that formation. I thought it was funny to see one goose nearly fly into the goose in front of it. It suddenly jerked its neck back and thrust its body and wings into a stopping motion. It was a near accident in the sky above me. Maybe that is why they are always honking.

I giggle at seeing cows close up. I think it is funny when people say that those cows are thinking something. They have those big eyes and that blank look. Do they even think? Like the look of concentration on a baby's face as food and gas pass through its digestive system, maybe the cows are merely staring blankly, chewing their cud, as the sensations of the food being processed and digested through their four stomachs consumes them.

I remember the cow with its fierce stance and its glaring gaze as though it were about to snort and charge. It was funny to me to see the dried, broad, maple leaf stuck to the bottom of its mouth as it threateningly followed my movements. Was it a menacing, ready-to-charge beast defending its ground or was it just a dull cow with a leaf stuck on its lower lip?

On one cycling journey, I watched a cow and a goose battle over and exchange territorial rights. There were three geese in a cow field along a small stream. A calf started down the long and steep hillside toward the stream. Because of the length and the steepness of the hill, the calf could not keep its legs from running to keep its top-heavy body upright as it descended. The calf was at the mercy of gravity, and it was barreling directly toward one of the geese. The goose's reaction was to take flight. As the goose averted its perceived danger, the calf, now free of its uncontrolled, descending motion of gravity, settled on the flat land beside the stream. It stood there in a normal cow-like stupor. The goose, however, wanted that grassy territory along the stream. It was circling back and with a highly agitated hissing and noisy commotion was descending for an attack. The hissing and honking goose put that little calf on the run –

running this time with fear from the dive-bombing goose.

As I cycle through farmlands, I like to watch cows walk. They bob their head up and down as though it is the piston of an engine, lifting and swinging each leg in its time, propelling their massive body forward. While I rested one day from hours of cycling, I watched Black Angus cattle moseying along a well-trodden path in a field. One cow was turned around facing the opposite direction of the herd. It just stood there in the path as another cow approached.

Next they had their heads butted against each other. They pushed forward and back several times with their heads locked together. For short periods they just stood still; they were probably resting their massive bodies. Eventually they would start forward and back again, spiral around to the side, and occasionally rest, but continuously with their heads pushed tightly against each other. Although the path was now clear, they continued. Finally, one cow pushed the other until it could not keep up with the pushing and pivoting of its huge body. Their headlock ended.

Funny though, now the two cows just stood there, like they did not know what had started their fierce activity. With the massive weight that they carry, they were probably exhausted. Both cows just stood there, looking confused. Neither one continued on the path. Eventually, each cow moseyed off in its new facing direction. There had been no purpose in it. Even more funny, was that it was a flat meadow. The entire field surrounded them with no obstructions to their passage. Either cow could have stepped off the path, and could have easily passed. That put a picture to the origins of the term, "bull-headed."

Once, I started a cattle stampede. A farmer had just delivered grain to the black and white dairy cows. They were all at the edge of the road with their heads stuck through the cattle fencing to eat from the grain trough. Several cows stopped eating and gazed at me as I neared. Like a combustion front, in one flowing tide, they each yanked their heads out of the feeding fence, turned, and ran far down and over to the distant side of their acres. Their behavior perfectly demonstrated herd mentality. I hoped that the farmer had not seen that I was the reason that they stampeded. It probably soured their milk that day. I do not know what I did that scared them. All I said was, "Hi cows." I was riding the recumbent then; maybe that was why they bolted in fear.

As I bicycle by the partial remains of an isolated foundation of what was ages ago a small home, I have time to reflect on who may have lived there. What was family life like then, living so far removed from any other homes, in that bygone day? I wonder why they left. While I crossed the prairie lands, I saw many recently vacated and boarded-up homes. I think of our current economic times and the impacts on those remote areas – the heart of our country.

Being attentive to, engaging in, and sensing the nuances of the nature all around you will lift your spirits. Let that nature permeate through you. Take in the shapes of the clouds. Do not miss a day knowing what the sky was like. Stop to eat the wild raspberries along the roadside. While you eat the cherries, blueberries, tomatoes, fresh breads, or whatever they have to offer at the local roadside produce stands, talk to the people. When they learn that you are bicycling across the country, you will influence their lives.

I love witnessing the reactions and comments from persons upon hearing that I am bicycling across the country. I often heard, "You are doing what?" I remember the motorcycle guy who said he tried, but could not cross the country on his motorcycle because it rained too much. Having already pedaled through days of downpours ourselves, we cyclists thought, "So?" There were several local residents whose eyes lit with dreamy imaginations and replied that they have never been out of their state. We inspire them.

My senses are aroused while I am pedaling out there, wrapped in nature, for many hours. The stimulated states intermingle and permeate within me. There is nothing pretentious about it. It is not a fantasy. It is not a movie production. These multiple stimulations are a genuine jubilation; they allow me to go deeper into my soul. My spirit is stirred and it cheers me. Yet in this complex intermingling of activity, within me is a mental and spiritual calm. There is an effect on my nervous system. There is tranquility and my mind can rest.

Best Shape Ever

I conclude the cross-country journeys in my best shape: physically, mentally and psychologically, and spiritually as well. Through the great demands on my body, I receive a huge spiritual reward, which balances my psychic consciousness.

The demands of cycling eighty-five miles every day optimize the cyclist's physical shape. The anatomical systems sustaining the strengthened, powerful muscles are optimized. The blood, lungs, cardio, respiratory, digestive, and nutritional systems are utilized to their maximum abilities. The cardiovascular system, from the heart to the tiniest capillaries, throbs vigorously. Muscles, tendons, and ligaments of the legs, arms, torso, and throughout the entire body are invigorated. The vibrant swelling and motion of all these systems engages hormones of the endocrine system. Bones, nerves, and skin are all enhanced by the stimulated energy production pulsating throughout the body. With the extensive hydration that the cyclist must receive, toxins are flushed out. We become full of vitality and exude vigor.

The stress of our normal lives is removed and replaced with a different kind of stress. The mental stress that I had created in going about my daily life and in driving that four-wheeled, commuter box is replaced by the physical stress of my throbbing quadriceps, calf, and shoulder muscles. Emotional stresses of grief, rejection, loss, or longing are replaced by excitement, gratitude, kindness, and forgiveness.

Subliminal senses of the mind are also stimulated. My capacity for perception, estimation, recognition, intuition, and comprehension seems to be heightened. These combined physical and mental senses meld and flow continuously in ever changing currents as they pour through me swirling in to replace the past. The various combinations create new, unique characteristics. It is like a symphony of senses throughout me. Like each instrument of an orchestra, each sense has its own vibration, and the infinite combinations, crescendos, intonations, reverberations, accentuations, harmonics, overtones, and vibrato produce the bliss and the lightness of spirit as the symphony plays within me. The compositions of these sensory inputs, ideas, and emotions switch off my head's self-generated noise and then go beyond that and drown out perverse exterior noises. The guy shouting something out his car window does not faze me. I interpret whatever he said as cheers of encouragement.

These cross-country rides have enhanced my self-awareness. I know my strengths and limitations better and have a stronger sense of my capabilities and self-worth. I have learned to regulate and manage my moods better. I handle emotions more favorably and keep disruptive impulses in check. I channel feelings into increasing my resourcefulness to enhance performance and productivity. I use emotions to propel myself into action toward my goals. Certainly these crossings required me to persevere despite obstacles and setbacks. This self-awareness, self-regulation, and self-motivation have boosted my self-confidence.

The simultaneous, splendid stimulation of all these senses stirs a spiritual vigor and vitality, which is enhanced and complemented by the physical and mental vigor and vitality. I am grateful to have these blessings. For me, cycling has been a personal, spiritual transformation. It is about being real. These coast-to-coast crossings have increased my self-confidence and pride, and I am filled with much more enthusiasm. Enthusiasm is derived from the Greek words "en theos," meaning having God within.

Bicycling across the country is a psychological challenge, but for me, it balances my body, mind, and soul. I have to think through my needs as I plan and organize before the tour. When the tour begins and pedaling becomes the primary event, however, I believe that it is best to embrace and undertake the challenge with pure emotion. I allow the sensations to permeate my being and do not analyze. I allow myself to feel these expressions of being alive.

From Sea to Sea

The vastness of the terrain across the United States is extraordinary, and the varieties of the sights are astonishingly abundant. There are not enough words, photographs, or videos that can arouse the emotions of the splendor and awe of being in any of the vast lands first hand. Our souls dance when we bask in those many marvelous skies, sunrises, and sunsets over land that goes beyond where our eyes can take us. Pictures stir our memories and emotions of when we were there. Photos, however, hardly express the magnificence to someone who has not been there. You must see those places for yourself. So go and broaden your horizons.

Whether the coast-to-coast bicyclist travels the northern tier, the central, or the southern route, the cyclist will experience the vastness and variety of this country. The routes have in common miles and miles and days and days of unsettled, rugged, open terrain. Even east of the Mississippi River, where the lands are more settled, the tour routes will cross long sections of rural farmland and forests devoid of urban development and housing. They all have this vastness in common, yet each route and nearly every state has its own distinguishing terrain. Each is a new experience of peerless treasures.

Mountains and Rocks

Perhaps a geologist could most appreciate bicycling across this country through his or her knowledge and awareness of the origins of land formations. There are many vast, rugged areas of nothing but mountains and rock. Yet the steep mountains in southern California are completely different from the brutal mountains and boulders of west Texas. Neither of them can be mistaken for the mountains of Nevada's vast, open, mountain plateaus and immense mineral-rich acres claimed by the Bureau of Land Management. The strange moonscapes of the Badlands are most distinctive in South Dakota. The solid granite mountain tops made famous by the carvings at Mount Rushmore and the Crazy Horse Memorial are unique to their area. In California, Yosemite's solid rock Half Dome and El Capitan are distinguished by their abrupt and astounding height. Only Utah has the colorful, mystifying geologic formations of abrupt bluffs and plateaus as showcased in Arches, Bryce Canyon, Zion, Canyonlands, and other national and state parks and preserved forest lands. Arizona has its share of rocks and mountains, but only in Arizona does the distinctive Saguaro Cactus dominate the landscape.

Pacific Coast

We can thank the foresight and influence of our twenty-sixth president, Theodore Roosevelt, and others with similar interest, for preserving open space along the Pacific Ocean. More than half the land along the Pacific Coast is preserved by land trusts, national and state forests, seashores, recreation areas, wildlife areas, preserves, sanctuaries, and parks. Farmland, wilderness, and other unsettled, public or government lands dominate the coastal lands. The American Dream of owning one's private piece of land does not include waterfront property there. Whether it is a large beach area or a small beach area, the surrounding sand dunes, cliff walls, farmlands, forests, scrub grass, and rural lands uniquely define each of these ocean front areas. Any favorite beach is distinct from a favorite neighboring beach.

The damp soil and moist, pine-scented air of the extensive forests of the Pacific Northwest define that area. Walking on the cushioned earth in those thick forests quickly fills one with that unique Pacific Northwest aroma not found in any other forests across the United States. The climates, terrain, and forests of the giant Sequoias of the Sierra Nevada Mountains are distinct from those of the Pacific Northwest, as they are likewise distinct from the Coastal Redwoods of Northern California.

Flowing from Canada, through Washington, and along the northern border of Oregon to the Pacific Ocean, the majestic, beautiful, and accessible Columbia River has no match of land formations and wide flowing river waters. Numerous splendid waterfalls along the Oregon side of the Gorge feed the river and define the region. Also unique to the Gorge are the open, regal, alluvial flows from mountains on the Washington side that pour in folds to the river below.

No other area of the United States matches the hills in Washington and Oregon, which flow with acres of fruit orchards. The springtime panorama when all the cherry, pear, and apple trees blossom on those undulating hillsides was gorgeous. Acres of pink cherry blossoms on one hillside, next to acres of white apple blossoms on another, next to a hillside of pink blossoms, flanked by another of white blossoms brought a beautiful sense of renewal.

Seattle is a bicyclist's dream city with hundreds of miles of paved trails around its waters and islands. The beach boardwalk of San Diego is completely different from the beach boardwalk of the Queen of Resorts in Atlantic City, New Jersey. In San Diego, we bicycled along while recalling scenes we had seen on the big screens and on our televisions. The historic wooden roller coaster added to the nostalgia, and of course, we had to take a ride on it to make the most of where we were.

Mountain Country

We bicycled along the shimmering calm waters of Idaho's Lake Pend Oreille and looked across to the far reaches of the mountains of the Coeur D'Alene National Forest. The extreme 1,150-foot depth of the glacial lake made it a submarine-testing site. The morning sun glistening on the water mesmerized like zillions of sparkling diamonds, and the crisp, clear air highlighted the beauty of the lake and its surroundings of abundant undeveloped forest. It was a splendid route to view the extensive timberland of Idaho's Northern Rocky Mountains.

Seeing Montana's distinctive wide-open, high-plains, with the flower-filled, green meadows reaching to the distant, timber-filled mountain ranges, with the crystal clear, blue sky above, explained why only this area is called Big Sky Country. Wyoming's vast terrain of grassy, rolling hills is perfect for admiring the grace and color of the antelope, other wild game, and the country over which they roam.

Traveling on our self-powered bicycles gives grand significance to the heights of the mountains. Overcoming the long, enduring climbs to the summits and passes leave us drained and exhausted. Yet with a brief rest, those sensations are quickly displaced by the exuberance of having achieved the climb to the top.

The steepest climb of my crossings was the climb over the 8,228-foot Emory Pass in New Mexico. Another memorable climb was surmounting the 11,312-foot Monarch Pass in Colorado. Our tour pedaled along with 2,000 other cyclists who were traveling the same route on the one-week Ride-the-Rockies tour. The difficulty of the climb was made more tolerable by having so many others struggling with me. The victory of reaching the top was made sweeter by the music, food, and festivities provided by the Ride-the-Rockies tour. Two thousand cyclists pedaling together to the top of an 11,312-foot pass is definitely a party.

The experience of bicycling the Going to the Sun Road to the 6,680-foot top of Logan Pass in Glacier National Park in northwest Montana evoked spiritual elation. Surrounded by the beauty of the glacial Lake McDonald and the waterfalls that feed it, the ride to the Glacier Peak above was celestial.

Each summit has its own memorable and spectacular views of its surroundings on the approach, the peak, and the descent. Each pass or summit – Soldier Summit, Snoqualmie Pass, Skykomish Pass, MacDonald Summit, Donner Pass, Mount Rose, Emory Pass, Emigrant Pass – has its distinct and unmistakable glory. Each view from the mountain to the valley below, unfolding to the horizon, was exuberating. The descent from the mountains of Nevada to the Salt Flats of Utah was a sweet ride. The road was smooth and the descent swift, but I stopped several times to absorb the scenery. The views across those immense Salt Flats were an inspiring spectacle – another one of a kind region. In the Appalachian Mountains, it was mystifying to see the thick fog flowing and sinking into the valleys between the reaches of the thick deciduous forests.

Rolling swiftly down hills is always fun. The fastest sustained speed that I have ever traveled on a bicycle is fifty mph. That was on my Litespeed on the eastern descent from Monarch Pass in Colorado. The second fastest was forty-eight mph on my Trek on the eastern, twelve-mile descent from MacDonald Pass into Helena, Montana. The highway surface was smooth, there were other cyclists traveling the road so motorized traffic was already alerted to our presence, and vehicle traffic was light. We claimed the right lane to have maneuvering room for avoiding road hazards.

Perhaps the thinner air at the higher altitude, which means less air resistance, makes these speeds possible. Perhaps it is the steepness of the grade, which is often most acute near the summit. Perhaps I had some tail wind. Regardless, it is exciting to move that fast on a bicycle. I remember my helmet being pulled back, my sunglasses pressed hard against my nose and brow, and teardrops flowing from the edges of my eyes because of the force of the wind. That speed is exhilarating, yet it is scary to be on such a small, open, thin machine. It is a body sensation unmatched by any amusement ride.

Although it was a smooth six-percent grade, the eight-mile-descent on Interstate-8 between Jacumba and Ocotillo, California was my slowest downhill ride. Sudden, extremely strong winds came bursting through the canyon to the right of us. We had to travel very slowly for fear of the winds blowing us into the interstate traffic. Several times I had to totally stop to stay in control and to be safe. The gusts were so intense and dangerous that some cyclists chose to be transported down in the SAG vehicles.

River Valleys

Each of our mighty rivers has its defining characteristics that distinguish it from the others. In its descent from Mount Hood, the Salmon River rushes with the freshness and youth of icy, blue-green glacial river waters and flits its path here and there through the Pacific Northwest timberlands. Certainly there is no comparison to the Colorado River's formation of the walls of the Grand Canyon. Wind surfers know the most perfect place for flying the winds is the incomparable Columbia River Gorge. The tiny, gentle Virgin River astounds us of its creation of the canyon at Zion. The Clark Fork River, train rails, and our roadway intertwining through an open, unsettled valley in Big Sky Country beautifully exemplified the open American frontier and our freedom to travel.

On our Southern Crossing, after many long, hot days of cycling across arid, boulder-strewn west Texas, I will forever remember the scenes and relief of the Frio River. We were as miserably parched as the soil, yet strangely in this arid land, there  flowed the shallow, thirty-foot wide Frio River. Almost all of us walked into the water and found a submerged rocky ledge where we just sat until our bodies could finally cool.

Each river has its identifying valley, and we are blessed in this nation with so many. Whether the Mississippi, Missouri, Arkansas, Wabash, Ohio, St. Lawrence, Savannah, Hudson, Delaware, Chattahoochee, or Suwannee, each served up distinctive routes, valleys, and memories.

Lakeshores

Lakes throughout this country are also each distinctive bodies of water. Attributes of the surrounding lands along with characteristics of the water itself define them. The encapsulating, forested mountains, abundance of snow, and excellent ski trails and facilities enhance the emerald green waters of the southwestern shores of Lake Tahoe. The peculiarities of such a large inland body of salt water as Utah's Great Salt Lake make it unique.

Each of the massive Great Lakes (Lake Huron, Lake Michigan, Lake Superior, Lake Erie, and Lake Ontario) are named starting with the word Lake to remind us that they are lakes and not seas. Each has a history of presenting tumultuous waters to challenge their navigators; stories are told of those who lost the challenge. Those lakeshores seem to be seashores extending out beyond the reaches of our vision. Indeed, residents of the central states vacation at these lake beaches as others do at the Atlantic and Pacific beaches.

Watching the fish many feet below in the clear depths of the glacial waters of Lake Chelan, Washington was delightful, but it was the surrounding orchard-filled hillsides that I found most spectacular. In Montana, the crystal clear lakes in Waterton Glacier International Peace Park slice through their surrounding dense forests, creating a paradise for wildlife and visitors. Another group of incredibly clear glacial lakes are New York's Finger Lakes with their distinct, steep hillsides of skillfully pruned, abundant grapevine cordons growing in uniform rows along the trellis wires. Seneca Lake claims the "Lake Trout Capital" title and is the destination for serious competition every Memorial Day weekend for the "National Lake Trout Derby." Twenty-pound lake trout are often hooked. When you travel into this area, treat yourself to an order of fresh lake trout.

Trains

Many of us are stirred by the allure of trains. They symbolize American industrialization, freedom, romance, and yearning to explore our vast lands. Unlike airplanes, which leave our earth for the heights above, trains stay here with us. They are not isolated from us by fences. We cross the tracks and travel with them. We can smash a penny on the rails. There is a mystique when they disappear into and appear out of a mountain tunnel or cross a bridge high over a ravine. As we bicycle across this country, with its rich variety of landscapes for backdrops, we have multiple opportunities to stir that fascination and be charmed by trains.

Plains States

The plains states have headwinds in common. They share the agricultural mindset of their independent, self-sufficient farmers. The heartland of Kansas is recognizable as we pass numerous cattle feed lots and high-rise grain mills, which supply the feed to make those cattle plump. South Dakota has its wheat grass, clover, and other dry grasses on terrain that undulates to the horizon. Farm homes and buildings are scarce, yet prairie dogs pop out of their holes monitoring activity, such as ours, as we talk while fixing a flat. Iowa has its mighty green hills climbing out of its lush river valleys. Away from those rivers, the wide-open fertile land of gradually rolling hills and valleys unfold to the horizons. Peppered across the landscape are the farm homes. Iowa is known for its pig farms, cornfields, pork chops, popcorn, and Blue Bell ice cream.

Southern States

Our Southern Crossing Tour was special for routing us on many back roads removed from the rushing traffic. In Louisiana, we traveled meandering roads along many waterways of the Mississippi Delta. Unique to that area is the slower, relaxed pace of folks and the drawl of their speech. They graced us with their genuine southern hospitality. When I was told that the large, round, domed, metal buildings were gator farm pits, I tended to pedal faster. I feared any gators that had strayed from their farm.

With thirty days of traveling across California, Arizona, New Mexico, and Texas, we had many meals of southwestern food. Corn, tomatoes, beans, avocados, rice, tortillas, tacos, enchiladas, burritos, flautas, salsa, and cilantro – we had eaten it all. In Louisiana, we transitioned to Cajun cuisine with jambalaya, gumbo, Cajun meatloaf, and Creole sauce. In New Orleans we had strawberry beignets and chicory coffee. In Florida, we ate scrumptious, fresh oysters.

Along the Gulf Coast of Mississippi, we bicycled by the beautiful and stately antebellum homes with their majestic plantation shade trees embellished with Spanish moss. In Biloxi, we experienced an evening at the casinos. Some took advantage of the urban setting to see the live stage show, "Stomp," which left us making music on any available can.

Florida has more than just sunshine to remember. The gentle waves and waters of the Gulf of Mexico allowed us to play in the fine, soft white sand of Florida's panhandle coast. For many, these outer coastal barrier banks are a favorite summer beach retreat. The Apalachicola pine forests made the region a lumber capital following the Civil War. Entrepreneurs in the lumber industry lived in magnificent homes along the coast. Today the leading industries are seafood canning and tourism. The Elgin Air Force Base and the

Pensacola Naval Air Station support the economy of the western panhandle also.

The town of Sopchoppy claims to be the "Worm Grunting Capital of the World." Gulf Coast fishing sports ensure the longevity of this skill. A large core of a sweet-gum tree trunk is driven into the loamy earth. The loud grunting noise is made when a large, heavy, metal bar is rubbed across the top of the shaped sweet gum spike. Whether it tickles or agitates, the audio or physical vibration makes worms actively twist and turn. It is rock and roll for worms. As they wiggle in response to the grunting, they show themselves in the soil, where they can be easily scooped up and put into the bait bucket.

West of Apalachicola, Florida, Forrest and I were bicycling along on a hot, humid, isolated stretch of marshland. Forrest wanted a soda. He had Gatorade. He had water, but he wanted a cola. There were no convenience stores. There were no gas stations. Along this stretch there was not much of anything: no buildings, no homes. A sign told of a campground located on a side road to our right. We turned off-route to go to the campground. After finally rounding the bend in the road, we still had not come to the campground, and I could see no driveways ahead. I said that was far enough. I did not want to continue farther off-route and still have to pedal back. It was hot, we had already pedaled sixty-five miles, and I was tired. We returned to our tour route.

We eventually came to a large, weatherworn, old, shack of a building that may have previously been a Mom and Pop grocery store. There was one car parked to its side. The remains of peeling paint on the sign above the porch read Indian Pass Raw Bar. The building looked abandoned, but it had a modern Pepsi sign on one of the pillars. We leaned our bikes along the posts, tried the door, which to my surprise opened, and walked in. By golly, it was packed! All the cars had been parked around the back, where we could not see them. At the many tables, happy vacationers and local residents were savoring local oysters. Forrest and I sat down. He had a Pepsi. I had ice cream. The waitress asked whether we wanted oysters. We answered no. Forrest and I discussed and agreed that neither of us had ever been excited about the oysters that we ate in the past. Yet, as we sat there, resting and recuperating in the air conditioning, wait-staff were bringing tray after tray of oysters to all the tables.

When in Rome, do as the Romans do. Forrest and I still did not think oysters would please our palates. We ordered just a half dozen. Wow! They were yummy! Perhaps it was their freshness. Perhaps Apalachicola oysters are especially delicious. Whatever the reason, we liked them and ordered a dozen more. We were having so much fun talking to the local folks and relaxing in the environment and savoring the oysters, we ordered another dozen. When we pedaled to camp, we heard that the staff had been worried about us. Everyone else had come in hours before, but we did not care. We were happy to have our special memorable day. When you are in Apalachicola, I recommend finding the Indian Pass Raw Bar and savoring the oysters.

Battlefields

Terrible battles have been fought on our soils. From the French and Indian War, the American Revolutionary War, the many battles and massacres of the Native American Nations, the War of 1812, the Texas Revolution, the Mexican-American War, the American Civil War, to our War on Terror, so many lives have been lost as our freedoms of today have been enabled and our vast lands have been claimed and defined. Exploring the many sites of those sad miseries while peacefully traveling on a bicycle incites deeper commemoration for the lives that were lost and for the reasons that the events transpired on those lands.

Unique Towns

Each town possesses its unmistakable, special identity and distinguishing features. The memories they stir are unique. San Francisco charms with its cable cars, the unique color of the Golden Gate Bridge, and the crisp Pacific air. There is no way I could pedal up those steep city hills. I would not want to ride down them either. I would worry about the brakes holding, and I would worry about flipping over the handlebars. The rows and rows of parking racks in Davis, California overflowed with bicycles. I would have had trouble finding where I had parked my bike if I had left it there for hours. I liked visiting some of the top-notch bike shops in Davis. Seattle, Washington has hundreds of miles of smooth, wide, paved paths around the many lakes and throughout the city. It is perfect for safe weekend recreation and also for commuting to work via bicycle. In Florida, the gentle waves and white, Gulf Coast sand in Panama City lured us into the water. Dodge City, Kansas still reenacts Gunsmoke. Away from the neon glare of the casinos in Winnemucca, Nevada, the rugged, old-west, expansive, openness sprawls to the mountains. San Antonio, Texas has several missions showing history of the area. Along the San Antonio River, we enjoyed the paved path, which we bicycled on to visit those missions. We relaxed on our walks to the Alamo and along the city River Walk. In Gettysburg Pennsylvania, we rode through many miles of hallowed ground, where numerous monuments mark maneuvers during the Civil War. Touring the site by bicycle was perfect.

James Edward Oglethorpe's foresight in 1742 positioned public squares throughout the grids of his colony. Today, Savannah,

Georgia has the distinction of having the largest National Historic Landmark district. Each of the twenty-four preserved and beautiful squares provides a park-like oasis. Majestic, moss-laden oak trees preserved through the ages hold sentry. Colonial residents of the wards surrounding each square chose and distinctly arranged their square's monuments, gardens, and trees. Today, each square is beautifully different from the others and instantly recognizable.

No other town has moose roaming the streets as they do in Bennington, Vermont. Only by being in Erie, Pennsylvania could one truly appreciate the many varieties of captivating frogs. Colorful creative crabs crawl along the sidewalks of Baltimore, Maryland. Only Washington, DC has the Lincoln Memorial, the Washington Monument, the Tidal Basin, the U.S. Capitol, the Reflecting Pools, the Jefferson Memorial, and the many other landmarks of this splendid nation.

American Dream

I liked seeing how individuals and families are living the American Dream. Homes vary tremendously from urban areas to the isolated rural areas. There are homesteads in some of the most rugged, dry, and rocky areas. There are houses on small plateaus with bluff drop-offs for yards. There are residences isolated deep in the forests and mountains.

Although some are loftier, many of the homes are very basic, but are what their owners can afford. Many claim and settle in acres of the barren outreaches of this nation, which are less expensive. Some settlements were small or in need of much repair, yet their owners have their freedom to do what they want with their property, and they have pride of owning that home. It is their American Dream. I cherished bicycling through so many varied areas of this country, seeing how others live, and seeing what the American Dream is for so many.

Traveling at Bicycle Speeds

We bicycled through Amish farmlands. The Amish have settled regions of Indiana, Ohio, Iowa, Illinois, Wisconsin, Delaware, Maryland, Kansas, as well as Pennsylvania. I would much rather travel through Amish country on a bicycle than in a car. I believe I am being less invasive and more respectful to their way of life.

Traveling on a bicycle is the perfect way to be aware of the land transitions across this nation: from the oceans to the mountains and from the wide open, dry prairie to the rolling hills and lush farmland. The United States has countless ecosystems from the Petrified Forests of Arizona to the Green Mountains of Vermont. Traveling at bicycle speeds, we are continually inundated with the majesty and beauty of our surroundings. Every day our senses are immersed in being there; we are intimately involved in the weather, the terrain, and the landscapes. We are in touch with our environment, and we experience the distinctions of one area from another. We are blessed to have such an extensive and multi-faceted nation.

We must stop occasionally and look around, look back, and listen to nature. We must be aware and watch the birds, the critters, and the crawling things that we are connected with. Whether it is on a large geological scale or on a small critter scale, whether on a short term or on an eternal term, there is life all around us. We are not a separate entity, but one with nature in the tremendously expansive and endless variety of these lands from sea to sea.

Shared Experiences

On each of my crossings, the tour company arranged the final, victorious ride to the Atlantic Ocean so that all of us rode together in a tight group. The enthusiasm was contagious. Negative emotions of sorrow, stress of everyday life, and fear of inadequate bicycling ability have been long gone. All of us cycling together, each wearing the same colors of our tour jerseys, piqued the blissful, ecstatic, and shared emotions. Words cannot describe the exuberant feelings. Our overt manifestation of blissful tears expressed the overpowering emotion and exaltation as we bicycled our last miles together.

For the past seven weeks these thirty people have shared the arduous, physical efforts, as well as the peaceful, easy rolling progress. They have persisted together and encouraged one another through the strenuous, difficult, painful, and exhaustive periods. They have shared the profuse emotions from dismal to euphoric. Together they have overcome the obstacles and challenges. They have shared the descents, the pacelines, their stories, the headwinds, the tailwinds, the climbs, the good and bad food, the special and disappointing lodgings, the rain, and the dehydrating, baking sun. They have shared the relaxation, achievement, adventure, social interaction, fitness, health, and well-being. The shared experiences will always bond the cyclists.

Our climb to the 11,312-foot top of Monarch Pass was a memorable challenge, which we surmounted together. No matter how low the gearing on our bicycles, it required strenuous effort to self-power the many miles of the ascent. With only a double chain-ring, I did not have low enough gears to spin more easily. I stopped every five minutes for forty-five seconds to calm my frenzied heart. With determination and persistence, I finally rolled to the top. As I approached, the other cyclists cheered enthusiastically, showered compliments, and embraced me with congratulatory hugs. We were high on a mountain.

As our tour continued, a gazillion other events occurred among our group. We lived together day and night for seven weeks sharing cycling and living experiences. Throughout the tour, we heard one another's stories and backgrounds. Many of the cyclists had the pleasure of their wives, husbands, boyfriends, girlfriends, or parents meeting with them at various times to share their elation and marvel at their accomplishments and perseverance.

Thirty-two days after surmounting Monarch Pass, we were in New Hampshire where we had our group celebration of our achievement of completing the 3,850-mile crossing. Many family and friends joined us as we celebrated. We each had our opportunity to speak our thoughts about the tour. I was thoroughly surprised to hear Doug Burleson of Odessa, Missouri say that my rolling to the top of Monarch Pass and the elated hugs of sharing that accomplishment was one of the experiences that he treasured the most. Until that celebratory day, I never thought my presence had any particular significance to him.

Bobbi Fisher from Burbank, California continually encouraged me and allowed me to draft behind her to complete the long, hot 112-mile ride from Aquila to Mesa, Arizona. As there was no time limit on when we finished, that must have been a low-pressure day for Bobbi. She is a member of the "California Double Century Hall of Fame." To achieve that distinguished membership, she had to complete fifty double centuries. Each of those one-day, two hundred mile rides had to be completed within a time limit, usually eighteen hours. That time is from start to finish. The clock does not stop for rest breaks, food stops, flats, muscle cramps, darkness, rain, or anything else. In addition to those combined 10,000 miles of endurance cycling, Bobbi has also completed the Odyssey 2000 Tour, which bicycled 365 days around the world. Bobbi says that she lives for double centuries. I am honored to have shared a crossing with her.

Christine Leininger from Coatesville, Pennsylvania, also encouraged, nudged, and pushed me to pedal farther and accomplish more than I would have without her prodding. She previously had bicycled coast to coast in twenty-eight days. Obviously, she can bicycle faster than me. She allowed me to draft behind her on the flatter roads and would wait for me along the climbs. Her soft words of encouragement persuaded me to continue cycling with her to complete the day's biking into Topeka, Kansas. It was very hot, and our route seemed to seek every climb within Topeka to take us to our motel. The reward was traveling by bicycle through Topeka's beautiful parks on our quiet, two wheels.

It was a pleasure to ride with older cyclists who inspired me. On my southern crossing, I became friends with Neil Van Steenbergen of Eugene, Oregon. On that coast-to-coast tour, Neil was seventy-five. Neil had just begun bicycling six years previously. He was lured to the sport by his desire to see the world at a slower pace. Neil is an inspiration to the baby boomers among us. In 1996, Neil learned about the Odyssey Bicycle Tour, which Tim Kneeland was organizing. It was a 365-day bicycling adventure around the world. It started January 1, 2000 with the cyclists riding in the Rose Bowl Parade. Touring the world at the speed of his self-powered bicycle sounded like a wonderful opportunity to Neil. At the age of sixty-nine, he bought a bicycle and started training. In 2000, at seventy-three, Neil bicycled around the world in 365 days on the Odyssey

Tour.

Also with us on the Southern Crossing was Jimmy Porter from Tacoma, Washington, who was seventy-one. With us on the Northern Crossing was Tony Quici from Roswell, New Mexico, who was seventy-eight. After cycling with us, he returned to Roswell to take trophies in the Senior Games. On my Central Crossing Tour, our oldest cyclist was Mel Siedman of Glen Cove, New York. Mel was seventy.

On the southern crossing, Shirl Kenney from Cedar Rapids, Iowa was our oldest female cyclist at sixty-seven. Shirl had also bicycled the Odyssey Tour in 2000. Neil and Shirl so enjoyed that experience and Tim Kneeland Tours that they had returned to do the Southern Crossing Tour with the TK&A organization.

Several sixty-something cyclists share the pride of pedaling from sea to shining sea. Those sexagenarian cyclists, whom I had the honor of crossing with were Ed and Bonnie Matson from Longview, Washington; Bill Cooley from Boulder, Colorado; George Carlson from Minneapolis, Minnesota; Terry Zmrhal from Arlington Heights, Illinois; Ann Yuhas from Brightwood, Oregon; Gerry Rawlings from Freeland, Washington; Bob Hollingsworth from Bellingham, Washington; and Bill Looney and Astrid Berg, both from Seattle, Washington. They each provide inspiration to all of us.

9

My Bicycles

I rode a different bicycle on each cross-country journey. All my bikes were road bikes with smooth rolling road or touring clincher tires. A mountain bike would definitely be inappropriate for one of these coast-to-coast rides, which cover an average of eighty-five miles a day on mostly asphalt roadways.

I know a few things about bicycle maintenance, but I often need a qualified bike mechanic. Little by little, I learn more about the science, engineering, specifications, and mechanics of precision, fine-tuned bicycles and their components.

P-38 Recumbent

My first crossing was on a Lightning, "P-38," short-wheelbase, above-seat-steering recumbent. A recumbent is a bike that has a backrest like a kitchen chair or perhaps more like a beach chair. Long-wheelbase means that the front wheel axle is ahead of the vertical of the pedals and crank arms. These are long, stretched machines. On a short-wheelbase recumbent, the pedals and the rider's feet are ahead of the front wheel. To the uninitiated, it could look strange to see this bicycle rolling down the road with pedal-spinning feet approaching and leading the way, ahead of the front wheel, with the rider sitting on top and reclining against the backrest.

I had been riding recumbent bicycles for seven years. My first was a short-wheelbase, under-seat-steering, Advanced Transportation Products "Vision." Next I owned an Easy Racer "Tour Easy," which is a long-wheelbase, above-seat-steering machine. I had bought it second hand, but it was a size medium/large and a bit too big for me. I sold both the Vision and the Tour Easy and bought an Easy Racer "Gold Rush," size small/medium, which fit me perfectly. Recumbent enthusiasts know its configuration. It is a long-wheelbase, above-seat-steering recumbent and conjures up images of the chopper motorcycle in the movie, "Easy Rider."

However, I took the P-38 on the coast-to-coast trip. Because it has a short-wheelbase, it was easier to ship it to the ride start. Also, it would be easier to haul if I needed or wanted SAG transport. It is a lightweight, fast recumbent and did a great job for me.

There are many things I liked about riding a recumbent bicycle. Instead of wearing tight, spandex pants, I wore short, loose-fitting, running shorts. Because it was like sitting in a beach lounge chair all day, I had the best tan during those years. The riding position was perfect for looking out, around, and up and taking in the sights. It was comfortable and easy to watch birds flying overhead or simply observe the cloud formations. Another advantage was the comfort level after eating. While riding my conventional upright bike, the leaning forward position caused my stomach to grumble and return food for reprocessing. That never happened on the recumbent bikes.

It was a long time before I adjusted to reclining and balancing on a recumbent. My first recumbent was a short-wheelbase, under-seat-steering machine, which has a twitchy steering response. My feet were high off the ground, which also made the adjustment more difficult. Like all of us, I am usually upright or leaning forward when I have to balance and do not think about balancing when I am reclined on a lounge chair.

For the first 200 miles of my riding on the recumbent, I thought I needed a seat belt. I thought if I hit a bump, I would bounce up and the recumbent would continue without me. I rode another 200 miles before I began to relax my upper body. Pulling up on the handlebars was not assisting my propulsion, but was making my shoulders tense. Eventually, I accepted that my legs had to do all the work of propelling the recumbent. Although I could exercise alternate muscle groups by pushing my shoulders against the backrest, it was still my legs that did all the work. I needed an additional 200 miles to recognize and mentally accept the reclined sense of balance. Finally, after those 600 miles, I began to feel "one" with it. Leaning back and balancing was a large part of the fun body sensations with recumbent cycling.

My favorite part of riding a recumbent was seeing the best smiles, because I was riding the funky thing. The reactions of others seeing me sitting on my lounge chair on top of the "bent," with my spinning feet leading the way as I rolled toward them, was refreshingly enthusiastic. I saw the best spontaneous smiles light up as soon as I was seen. The arousal of gleeful laughter was a common reaction to seeing me on that strange thing. I so enjoyed the light-hearted reactions at my sight. Kids excitedly would shout, "I want a bike like that!" I had lots of fun and attention over the years while I rode recumbent bikes.

I was the only recumbent rider on my first cross-country ride. The physical dynamics of cycling on a recumbent are different than cycling on a conventional bike. It can be difficult to match pace between the two as the terrain changes. Situations along the journey made me think about trading the bent for a conventional bike.

Over the first twenty-five days from our start at the west coast, strong bonds were formed between cyclists. These ties deepened with our shared experiences: our difficult challenges, victorious achievements, cycling in tandem, conversing over meals, and enjoying the evening entertainments. I think that many of us also began to consider that this wonderful adventure would soon be coming to an end. We wanted to ride together and share our remaining experiences.

East of San Antonio, Texas, our route traveled many miles of predominantly flat terrain. Also, we had been pushing into a steady, firm headwind from the southeast that stayed with us every day across Texas. The combination of the flatter terrain, the steady headwinds, and the bonds that we had formed prompted us to develop pacelines.

When I rode the recumbent in the slipstream, I was not acquiring as much draft assistance as the upright cyclists were able to obtain. On my recumbent, I had to be dangerously close to the cyclist ahead of me for a beneficial assist. On an upright bike, I did not need to be so close to the cyclist ahead to feel that assist. I could allow a gap while I looked around or took a drink. When I needed to shorten the gap, I could easily accelerate ahead.

I remember on the recumbent always having to pedal so hard. I was constantly watching the cyclist and bike ahead of me in order to stay close enough to stay with the paceline. Every day, when the road came to a gentle rise, due to a bridge or a large sand dune, I could not keep up with the other cyclists. The upright cyclists have the definite advantage of being able to easily and quickly accelerate. This ability is translated into maintaining the paceline speeds on those short ascents. On the recumbent, I could not muster that acceleration. I would slide right off the end of the paceline.

The cyclists in the paceline would slow for me so that I could catch up with them. However, after working so hard on the climb and working so hard to catch them, I would be exhausted. Bicyclists know that being any place in a swift paceline is work. With concentrated effort, I could stay with them for many miles, but I had to accept that I could not continue with those upright cyclists when there were ascents, even the short ones. Eventually, I would have to ease off and tell them to keep going without me. That happened every day!

That frustration provided the incentive and motivated me to make the switch to riding an upright, conventional bike. Practicing yoga for three years was key to enabling me to make that transition. Yoga made me learn to pivot my torso forward at the hip and pelvis. It taught me to keep my back, torso, spine, neck, and head in a straight line. Bobbi Fisher from Burbank, California succinctly advised, "Use your abdominal muscles to hold your torso." Great advice that I tell myself often.

Trek WSD

On my northern crossing I rode a brand new Trek 2300,

conventional-frame, road bike. It was a 49cm Women's Specific Design (WSD) with 650c wheels. The smaller wheels reduced the reach from the seat to the handlebars for women, who often have shorter torsos than men. It was a perfect bike for transitioning my body from seven years of recumbent cycling to riding a traditional upright bicycle. I loved it. I expected that I would ride it well into my senior years. When I could no longer power up the climbs, I would put a motor on it. When I could no longer keep my balance, I would put training wheels on it. When Jeff Schleiper said that it was too small for me and that I would outgrow it, I disagreed. No way! This WSD bike fit me perfectly – I thought.

I was completely comfortable on it. I pedaled it every inch from Seattle, Washington to Chambersburg, Pennsylvania. I rode it over the Cascades, the Rockies, through the Black Hills, the Bad Lands, across the Central Plains, through the congestion around Chicago, and over the Appalachians. On our forty-fifth day, I had already pedaled eighty-five miles from that morning's start in Bedford, Pennsylvania. On a gently rising grade into Chambersburg, it died. I was baffled why the pedals locked up. They would no longer spin. I got off and looked at it. Things looked confusing around the rear-wheel hub. I had not remembered it looking that way before. The confusion cleared as I stared at what was in front of me. The rear derailleur was above the hub, instead of below, where I had been accustomed to seeing it.

Since I did not have a cell phone, I walked to several homes until I found a friendly couple that permitted me to use their telephone to call the tour mechanic. The mechanic showed me how the frame had broken in the back triangle corner where the chain stay and the seat stay come together. This is where the rear wheel axle connects to the bike frame and where the derailleur and derailleur hanger attaches. The broken frame allowed the normal spring force to pull the derailleur farther inward, where it was snatched up by a spinning spoke that rotated it to that strange position above the hub, making the chain bind up around the rear cogs. The mechanic told me that he could not fix it. I borrowed a bike to finish the next and final two days of the tour from Gettysburg into Washington, DC.

Because the aluminum bike frame could not be welded, the frame was junk. I had to decide whether to buy a new replacement frame of the same size or step up one size. The loaner bike was the next bigger size and not a Women's Specific Design. Pedaling across the country had given me a very bicycle fit body; I was comfortable on the larger, loaner bicycle. During the crossing, I wanted to stretch my body out for better cycling comfort and strength. With the smaller WSD bike, I continually wanted to raise the saddle to allow that stretched, extended body space. That, however, is the wrong way to obtain that stretch as my hips were rocking with every pedal rotation. Not good. The better way was for me to be on a larger bike frame to allow stretching my torso and spine. Jeff had been right! That bike was too small for me.

By the time that I returned the Trek to my local bike shop, it had been thirteen months since I had purchased it. As the one-year factory warranty had just expired, Trek would not replace the frame under warranty; I had to pay for the replacement frame. I had to decide whether to buy another 49cm WSD bike with the 650c wheel set or take the leap to the next size frame. I took the leap. My expenses grew, because the larger frame uses 700c wheels. In addition to buying the replacement frame, I had to buy new wheels, spokes, tires, and tubes. Of course, I paid for the excellent skills of Ray Clark from Frederick, Maryland to build these new wheels reusing the hubs of the original bike. The bill also included the labor to transfer the shifting, braking and drive-train components from the original bike.

Funny how things happen sometimes. It was probably best that I was forced to the larger bike. Now I can stretch my spine and torso out on the new bike. I do not want to raise the saddle to produce more power from my legs and body. I thought that with more cycling and more conditioning, I would stretch my body out even more. Perhaps I would even adjust my bicycle like the racers have theirs, with the handlebars set much lower than the seat. My next coast-to-coast cycling tour taught me that I have reached the limit of my torso stretching. With age, my handlebars are more likely to be adjusted up, rather than down.

Litespeed Ultimate

On my third crossing, I rode a 1999 Litespeed Ultimate, which I bought second hand on eBay. Upon finishing my second crossing, I had a very bicycle fit body, but no bicycle to ride. I had to wait for the new frame to come from Trek. Because I was in a frenzy to have a bike to ride, I turned to eBay where I found the Litespeed. I am its third owner.

The previous owners must have hammered the drive train. The chain-rings had to be straightened. Several of the spoke threads were stripped, and the rear wheel would not stay true. The wheel must have been warped because it would not come true even with replacement spokes. The wheel had to be replaced. The chain was stretched and needed to be replaced. The 11-23 cog-set was too demanding for my non-racer abilities and the hilly farm country where I live and ride. I replaced it with a 12-27 cog-set.

With thoughts of pedaling this bicycle across the central crossing, I worried about climbing the western mountains. It was now set up with the 12-27 cog-set and double 53/39 chain-rings. Converting it to a triple at that time would have cost more than $1200, just for parts. For those who do not know, the conversion requires purchasing the triple chain-ring crank-set; plus a wider bottom bracket to accommodate the wider, three-ring set; a new front derailleur for the three-ring wider movement; a new shifter lever for the three steps; plus a new longer rear derailleur to take up the chain slack created when in the low granny gear. The Litespeed's existing components were (top-of-the-line) Shimano DuraAce, and I wanted to stay with DuraAce for the triple components. This was after all, a high-end, expensive, titanium Litespeed.

The $1200 price tag on that conversion was too big for me to swallow. I discussed the compact crank solution with Ray Clark, my mechanic at Wheel Base in Frederick, Maryland. Ray proposed changing the rear cog-set to an 11-32. Ray's experience and skills have often enabled him to push Shimano's specifications and dependent on the bike frame, adjust the rear derailleur to accommodate the wider range cog-set. This solution was only $75.

For those who know gear inches, the 11-32 cog-set would give the bike 33.6" on the low end and 132.8" at the high end. That sounded better to me than the compact crank-set solution, which would give me 34.7" on the low end, but only 115" on the high end. In my book, the difference of 33.6" for the $75, 11-32 cog-set solution, versus the 34.7" low for the $300, compact crank solution was not worth my spending the $225 difference. Also, I did not like losing high-gear inches. I like going fast when I can. The original set-up on the Litespeed was a 121.7" high gear. The compact crank solution would have dropped that down to 115 inches.

I told Ray to change the cog-set to the 11-32. The bike then had a high of 132.8 gear inches. Ray was trying to save me money, but could not tweak the rear derailleur to work with the 11-32 rear and 53/39 front combination. I had to buy a new Shimano Deore XT long-throw, rear derailleur at a cost of $72. The combined cost of the rear derailleur and the 11-32 cog-set at $147 was still less than buying the $300 compact crank set. I rode the bike locally and took it on some climbs. They seemed easier than they had been before. I thought that I would be fine crossing the country with this double set up. I was not.

I am not a fast or strong bicyclist. My climbing abilities are weak and I pedal uphill very slowly. The muscles in my legs become sore quickly. The climbs were terribly demanding. Now I recommend a triple set up for everyone, always, everywhere. The climbs will be less strenuous. The ultra-low gear on the triple can help avoid knee injury when the climbs just will not end.

Since completing my third crossing, I was fortunate to purchase a new Shimano DuraAce 9-speed, 53/39/30 triple crank-set, triple bottom bracket, triple front derailleur, and triple front shifter for $300. The 9-speed triples are being replaced by Shimano's new 10-speed components. I installed the components myself, or at least, I installed them until I no longer knew what to do and why things were not working correctly. Then I humbly took the bike with the half-installed components to Ray, who finalized and perfected the installation. Now the bike has an ultra low of 26 gear inches and a high of 132.8." I have also  changed the handlebar stem from a 100cm to an 80cm. I am very comfortable on it, and I am trying to be stronger on the climbs. I would love to try this Litespeed triple set-up on another coast-to-coast ride.

10

Packing and Planning

Packing List:

Bicycle	Sunglasses
Helmet	Sunscreen
Mirror	Chamois cream
Cycling gloves	Wet Ones
Cycling sandals	Bike Lock
Cycling shorts (2 pr)	Map holder
Sports bras (2 pr)	ID, Medical Information
Tank tops (2 pr)	Camera
Money	Dry bag for camera

That is everything I need to pack for bicycling across the United States in the middle of summer. However, I we will be out there for two months and at times in high elevations so I need to pack some cold weather clothing.

Cold Weather Cycling Clothes:

Bicycling jersey	Poly fleece vest
Arm warmers	Rain Jacket
Leg warmers or tights	Rain Pants
High-Visibility Jacket	Full finger gloves
Bandanas (2)	Rain shoe covers
Socks	Balaclava
Cycling Shoes	

Many mornings will be cold and I will want much of this clothing. As the day and my body warm, I will be shedding the cold-weather clothes. To carry all the layers that I shed, I use curly shoestrings. I love these things. On my southern crossing trip, Forrest Roberts introduced me to their practical simplicity. I pull a  loop from the center of a string through the rear of one of the rails of my bicycle seat. I pull both ends of that string through the loop, pull the ends tight to close up the loop, and leave both curly ends hanging loose. One string is on the right rail. The other curly string is on the left saddle rail. It is amazing how much of my clothing I can roll up and secure with those curly shoestrings; it looks like the bedding rolls the cowboys tie to the back of their saddles. This method of carrying my extra clothing is fantastic because I do not add the weight of a rack and an extra bag to my bicycle. An extra bag tempts me to put things in it; then I carry the extra weight of things I rarely use.

On rainy days the wheel splash would make my rolled up clothes dirty. Now I put everything into a small, lightweight, nylon "dry bag." Dry bags are what kayakers use. I tie the tightly rolled dry bag bundle at the back of my seat with the curly shoestrings. It is efficient simplicity, and I love that.

Early Preparation

As for what to pack and what to bring, I suggest to start early. Many weeks before the start of your trip, make a list of every item you think that you will want while you are bicycling and living out there. Think of things you use throughout your regular day and whether you will want those things while on your trip: vitamins, medications, toothpaste, etc. Think of things you could need while pedaling miles on your bike, like spare tubes, tires, and spokes. Making this list is part of your dreaming of your adventure soon to be realized. Weeks before the trip, I start laying out every thing I want to take. This is where many advise to remove half.

As the next days unfold, I usually think of other little things I will want, such as a pocket-sized journal, stamps, addresses, phone numbers, traveler's checks, a larger spare memory card for my digital camera, batteries, chargers. By starting early, I will have time to acquire things I do not have. Sometimes, things that I had planned to take, need to be replaced. I really love the pads on those bike shorts, but the spandex has worn thin and my skin shows through. Time to charge more on the credit card and buy a new pair. Through the days I think of additional things, like who will pick up my mail or I remember another bill that will have to be paid while I am gone.

Bring only two pairs of after-ride street clothes. You will wear them so little in the evening that they will stay clean many days. You will put them on after you take a shower and wear them only a few hours each day. You will be too exhausted for ambitious activities that will soil them. Assuming that you do not wear your dinner or the chocolate from that ice cream, they will stay clean for many evenings. When you come in, tired and dirty from cycling all day, you will be glad you can quickly locate your clothes and go to the shower without having to think about what you are going to wear. Everyone will be too exhausted to much care about your fashion statements. Be certain to select clothes that are durable, washable, dry quickly, and most importantly, are extremely comfortable in every imaginable way.

Each of the cross-country tour companies had given us addresses where we could receive mail along the route. We had these addresses weeks before the tour started. Give a copy to each of your friends, relatives, and associates. You will love receiving greetings from them while you are off in your other world. Another use for these addresses might be for you to receive pre-planned care packages from yourself. Rather than pack your suitcase from the beginning with all the toiletries to meet your needs from start to finish, you could pack half. Box up the other half and have a friend mail it to the tour by a date that you specify. Be sure that it is mailed early enough for it to arrive before you do. You could restock your needs at stores along the route, and it is good to support the local economy wherever you are. This is assuming, however, that you will have time and that the store will be near to your overnight location when you need it.

Cycling Clothes

As for the cycling clothes, you will wash those out every night by hand. You could wear the other pair if the first pair has not dried completely or for variety. Some people carry liquid Woolite for washing. Travel-sized, 0.25-ounce Woolite packets are available at travel stores and on-line. Some carry their own rubber sink stopper, which is often needed at camping facilities. After you wash your clothes, wring them out several times as tightly as you can. Lay them on a towel and roll them and the towel up tightly. Wring that several times. You could unroll the towel and your clothes, move the clothes around, and roll them and wring them in the towel again. This will remove more moisture to better enable your clothes to dry completely over night. You really want your clothes to be dry by the morning when you must either wear them or pack them in your duffel. If you pack them when they are wet, they may become mildew smelling by the time you unpack them. That smell may migrate to the other things in your bag.

Bill Berendsen of Byron Center, Michigan carried in his duffel a lightweight, plastic, AC-powered fan that he purchased at a dollar store. After he washed and wrung his clothes, he hung them on hangers, and clamped the fan on to blow across them all night. His clothes were always dry in the morning. To stave off the reeking odor that they can develop, wash those gloves every couple of days too. I start the tour with clean cycling shoes. By the end of the seven-week tour they stink. I clean and refresh them by soaking them for an hour or two in a bucket of water with several capfuls of Lysol added.

As for the cycling shorts, it is important that the two pairs be different brands with different padding shapes. With day after day, week after week of cycling, chafing is likely to develop. By changing bike short brands and pads, you are less apt to continuously chafe the same locations. Any area that does chafe can have a respite the following day while you wear the other pair.

Be prepared that the jerseys or tank tops that you bring may become quite grimy by the end of your journey. Wearing and washing them every other day takes a toll on them. Some of the overnight locations have terribly hard water that just does not clean well and leaves garments grungy. Every day you will be lathering protective sunscreen on two or three times a day. Plus you will sweat profusely. Your lathered, glistening body sucks up the dirt, dust, and grime blowing across the land. The pollution from cars and trucks, plus the dirt that they stir up, will be hovering in the air. All the grime thrown into your path will stay with you until you take a shower. That grime will also be all over your cycling clothes every day.

There are days when you have to ride on wet roads. The oil droplets deposited by the vehicles on the previous dry days mix with the water. As you bike through it, your tires slush it right up on you and your clothes. This oily, sticky grime does not wash out easily, sometimes never at all. I was embarrassed at how filthy the washcloth became in the shower from scrubbing me clean after one of those wet, grimy days.

In Missouri, we bicycled through miles of sticky, wet, pebbly asphalt that tenaciously stuck to everything. After another twenty miles of cycling on "clean" roads, the asphalt still clung to our tires, bikes, clothes, and skin. The tires had to be forcibly scraped with a heavy, metal straightedge to remove the tar. We had to work the tenacious, sticky goop, and dried, hardened coatings off our bikes with oils and oil-based cleaners that could emulsify the gunk, yet not damage our bike's paint. We went through every old rag the motel could scrape up. The tar that was on my clothes has never washed out.

I like the utility of bandanas. On hot days I use one to soak my head and neck with water. On cold days I fold one into a triangle and tie it to cover and keep my head and ears warm. As the day warms, I can moderate my temperature by pushing it above my earlobes. When the weather is warmer, I pull it off and out from under the back of my helmet while I am cycling. In cold weather, I fold another bandana into a triangle, put the center of the fold over my nose, and tie it loosely behind my neck. The looseness allows me to easily turn my head and makes it quick and easy to pull over (or lower from) my nose when I need it. My breath warms the space it contains and keeps my cheeks and nose warm without fogging my glasses. When it is very cold, as it was for my central crossing going over the Sierra Nevada Mountains, a thin polypropylene balaclava is warmer than bandanas, and it packs easily.

I now also pack a pair of thin poly fleece full finger gloves that I pull on over my cycling gloves. They provide just a bit more warmth when needed for otherwise summer cycling. I do not own waterproof, cycling gloves for soaking rain days. If I am not on a tour, I will not be cycling in the rain. On trips, I now pack a pair of

Nitrile first aid gloves. Besides being waterproof, these also double to provide more warmth.

As for rain shoe covers, on my budget I just use plastic bags and rubber bands to cover my socks to try to keep my feet dry. I let my shoes be wet. When you are riding in heavy to moderate rain all day, your feet will become wet regardless of what you wear. I carry another pair of dry socks with me on the bike to change into along the ride. If you own cycling booties, pack them.

Additional Cycling Needs

You will definitely need sunscreen. Too many of the available lotions seal my skin and contribute to raising my body temperature. My pores are blocked, and my skin cannot breathe. Since I have difficulty with the heat, I need to use the liquid sprays. I like Coppertone Sport Ultra sweat-proof, sun-block, liquid spray. It is waterproof and provides SPF 30, UVA, and UVB protection. Another one that I like is Hawaiian Tropic Ozone Sport sun-block spray. It claims to be non-migrating, sweat-proof, and waterproof, and provides 30+SPF protection. Both of these liquid sunscreens are sometimes hard to find. The evaporating gels have worked best for me, but they are even more difficult to find.

I bicycle with a seventy-ounce Camelbak hydration pack. It is easier for me to drink more with it, but I have to stop more to drain the excess water. Hey, they say drinking lots of water is healthful. I put only water into the Camelbak. By putting only water into it, bacterial growth is minimized. Previously, I put Gatorade, PowerAde, Lemonade, or Iced Tea into my Camelbak. Then I saw slime growing inside the hose and nestled into the seams. Now that I have removed that and bleached the bladder, I do not want to risk having bacteria in there. I still clean and disinfect it periodically to minimize any dangerous growth in it. Camelbak's newer bladders advertise Hydroguard Anti Microbial Technology that eliminates 99.9% of all bacteria. That 0.1% started to grow in mine. Don't let that 0.1% make you ill.

On the cross-country tours, I carry the hose cleaning brush in my duffel. Efferdent comes in little packages that travel well and can be used in the evening to clean out the Camelbak and bottles. Water bottles can be scrubbed out easily or they can simply be thrown away and replaced with a safe, clean, new one.

My bike holds two water bottles. I put the Gatorade, PowerAde, or whichever sports hydrations drink in one. In the other, I put Perpetuem Extreme Endurance Fuel to aid my muscles. On those extremely hot days, I often fill one of the bottles with water that I use to pour over my head, neck, and back to lower my body temperature. Electrolyte capsules also help keep me hydrated. I always carry them, and on the hot days, I take them regularly. My favorite is Hammer Nutrition's Endurolytes.

When I am out there all day, I have to drink Gatorade, PowerAde, some other sports drink, or take electrolyte capsules to replace the salts and minerals my body sweats out. Drinking water only, even lots of it, does not always prevent heat exhaustion. I know from experience. I was feeling weak and had no energy. People told me to drink more water and I did. When I finally made it to camp, I was faint and dizzy. I parked my bike and went straight to the shower. I drenched myself, with my clothes still on, for ten minutes trying to cool down. My body was lacking needed electrolytes, but the water alone could not provide them. I was still exhausted that night.

On the other hand, one summer I drank nothing but the sports drinks in place of water for hydration. I gained five pounds, and nothing else about my eating or activity habits had changed. Now I drink half water and half sports drink. The balance of electrolytes in our bodies is vital.

There are a few other miscellaneous things I carry in my duffel. I carry a large tube or tub of quality chamois cream. I will be bicycling across vast distances of this country where there will not be any bike shops. Some small shops do not stock chamois cream. I carry several tubes of Neosporin. To alleviate the burn in my legs from the demands I make on them, I also carry Vanishing Scent Ben Gay or BioFreeze pain relieving gel. I choose the Vanishing Scent because I think that no one else need smell it. These provide muscle relief in the evening. I also apply the pain relieving gel to sooth my legs during the day while I am cycling.

A few shower caps can be very useful. When my bicycle has to stay outside overnight, I use one to cover the saddle and another one to cover the pads of my aero bars. When I must bicycle in a moderate or heavy downpour, I wear the shower cap on my head.

Financial Surprises

It is best to be somewhat prepared for additional expenses along the way. On one crossing, one of the cyclists bought two new top-quality wheels. On another coast-to-coast ride, the mechanic spent hours and hours on many days repeatedly balancing and making a rear wheel true. It probably should have been replaced, but wheels can be expensive. Some mechanics might not have been so patient. One cyclist had to replace a cog-set and chain, which probably should have been replaced before coming to the start of the tour. Along the tour route it may be difficult to locate a bike shop that sells particular components.

After Bill Looney rode two days on the Southern Crossing Tour, he decided his bike was not what he wanted to cross the United States on. He purchased a new bicycle for completing the tour.

Some of us received medical or dental surprises. One dealt with a urinary tract infection. Another needed a medical facility to lance an egg-size boil from his groin. I spent over $120 on better cycling shorts. Replacing my tooth for my cosmopolitan smile was nearly $200. Replacing the broken Trek frame set me back over $1,000.

Evening Gear

Our modern age brings with it our need for electronics. The cell phone needs its charger. The camera will need its charger or extra batteries and additional camera memory cards. I like having background music; my ipod (and charger) is essential. I like having it to fall asleep with, and I recommend the remote control adapter. I carry a small dry bag on the bike for these electronics. Dry bags are what kayakers put their gear in and can be purchased at kayak outfitting stores. I have a larger dry bag for the electronics I keep in my luggage, especially when I am tenting.

A small, lightweight, low-bulk journal is probably adequate. There will be little time for any more than a few notes to remember the day. I may write whether it rained or was sunny, the relaxed, easy pace afforded by the descent or the tailwind, the conversation I had with one of the other cyclists or with the locals at one of the stops. Perhaps I will note the triumph of ascending the summit, the terrain I pedaled across, or homes, trees, rocks, or water that stirred my emotions. Some simply write on the route sheets. Keep the writing brief. Just write the bullet items. It is more important to prioritize time to socialize with the other cyclists and make the most of sharing the adventure.

Having considered all these things, I try to pack less and not buy more unless it is absolutely needed. The less there is, the easier it will be to quickly pack it all and more easily remember and know that I have it all. I developed the practice that every time before leaving an overnight location or a rest stop, I look around for anything that was set down. No one wants to leave a cell phone; journal; jacket; the shorts, which were left out to dry; or anything else. We will have enough bicycling miles without having to pedal back for something that we forgot.

Cycling Equipment

For the bicycle, I recommend a comfortable road or touring bike with a triple chain-ring set. On the climbs a double set requires the cyclist to work muscles in the anaerobic range, which leads to more muscle soreness. With a triple, one can work muscles in the aerobic range rather than having to push the large gears. It will be easier on the cyclist's heart and knees. The body still has to do the work, but it will be better able to endure. To train, I recommend building climbing legs. If the cyclist lives along the eastern or southern shores, they may have to ride over a lot of bridges.

Carry a good frame pump. Each of my bikes always has a pump on it. Carry at least one spare tube. Out west, it is best to carry two spare tubes. The thorns, retread-tire wires, and glass debris hide camouflaged on the roadway shoulders waiting for the moment of their rebirth when they find the bicycle tire. Pack tweezers or miniature pliers to pull wires or thorns out of the tire rubber. Carry tire levers and a patch kit with patches the correct size for the road tires. Before a coast-to-coast trip, buy a new patch kit to ensure that the glue is fresh. Also carry a tire sidewall or boot patch.

I have a tool bag on each of my bikes. I use one of those little bags that strap on under the seat. My favorites are the Izumi Tailgate and Topeak's Micro Aero Wedge Pack. The tool bag contains a flexible spare spoke and a spoke wrench of the proper size to fit my bike's spokes. Once my seat bolt broke and I had to ride with the saddle at its lowest height. Since then, I stock my tool bag with the correct size seat clamp and bolt for that bike. This bag is only for repairs. I also stuff shower caps and Nitrile gloves for rainy weather in there.

There have been cyclists on these crossings that have never changed a tire by themselves. Some have changed a few, but it takes them a long time. That is okay. It would be better if they knew and could efficiently change a tire or tube. They will learn as the days go on. Since the cyclist should know how to change a flat tire, they should practice in the comfort of their home before the tour. The front tire is easier to take on and off and is usually cleaner to handle.

Thorns from prickly plants can cause flats, as can glass and debris along the highways. Sharp metal edges inside the rim where the spokes are attached can cause flats. Those metal edges must be covered by quality rim tape to protect that high-pressure tube.  Good rim tape provides protection surrounding the hole where the valve stem goes through the rim too. Retread tire debris from the 18-wheeler tractor-trailers is probably the most insidious enemy for causing flats. Retread debris is everywhere on the highways in the western and plains states. The extremely high speeds of the trucks on the long, straight highways contribute to those truck tires exploding. The hot, dry weather and sun-baked roads also contribute to their shredding. Additionally, there is too little rainfall to wash the debris off the roadway. Cyclists must try to avoid that truck tire debris. The tiny pieces of piercing wires from the reinforcement cords work their way into bicycle tires like one-way barbs. The source of the flat must be removed when the tube is changed. A thorn, glass, or wire that is not located and removed will flatten the new tube very soon.

The proper selection of tires can minimize punctures. Do not use race tires for a coast-to-coast ride. The rubber compound picks up road debris and holds on to it. This allows glass, thorns, and wires to work into and through the tire to the tube. Touring tires are better. Kevlar belted tires are best. Do not be confused by the term Kevlar bead. That refers to only the inner edge of the tire that seats against the rim. Kevlar beads have been an improvement in bicycle tires over the metal beads used previously. Prior to installation, the metal beads could be kinked and then would not completely seal to the rim. The biggest advantage perhaps to the Kevlar beaded tire was that the tire could be folded, thus enabling easier packing and storage. The Kevlar beaded tire is also lighter. However, it is the Kevlar belt that is key to minimizing flats.

An alternative to a Kevlar-belted tire is a Kevlar liner that is placed between the tire and tube. These are lightweight and thin. They provide protection along the rolling surface but none to the sidewall. Mr. Tuffy brand plastic liners are also available. They are bulkier and weigh more than the Kevlar liners, but they are less expensive, and they are indestructible. I was surprised to find that the Kevlar liners, which had been in my tires for several years, had separated in several places. In those gaps, there was no protection from thorns, wires, or glass causing a flat. The Mr. Tuffy liners are wider than the Kevlar and provide protection along a bit more of the sidewall. The correct liner width must be used to match the tire width. Otherwise, the liner could pinch the tube and cause a flat. On my 20" front recumbent tire, I cut the liner to shorten it to eliminate excessive overlap. Some cyclists who need the latest lightweight gear and always want to push their riding abilities to go faster, do not like adding the extra liner weight to the wheel. Sometimes I pass them while they are changing tires!

Thanks to modern technology, more and more tires are available with Kevlar belts molded into the rubber tread and sidewall. One of the first popular tires to have this feature is the Armadillo by Specialized. Most other manufacturers now also offer similar tires. Continental has Kevlar belts molded into their Ultra Gatorskin and Grand Prix tires. Michelin offers the Erilium Axial tire. My preference is the Continental Grand Prix Four Season. It is a high mileage tire with very good puncture resistance. Neil Sardiñas rode coast to coast with Mr. Tuffy liners inside his Armadillo tires. He never had a flat.

I recommend that the tires not be over inflated beyond the sidewall's maximum inflation rating. This is most critical on very hot days. As the outside temperature rises, also the pressure inside that tube rises. A small impact may be amplified when the pressure is too extreme and burst the sidewall. An instantaneous flat will demand your attention at the most unprepared and shocking moments. A fast moving bicycle that acquires an instant flat can be nearly uncontrollable, especially when it is the front tire.

Be comfortable shifting the gears on the bike. I write this because on one of my rides a cyclist rode nearly half of the crossing often in a non-optimum gear. Perhaps her hands were too small to press the lever firmly enough to affect the shift. I do not know. She just kept pedaling. If she was going up hill and her bike was in a high gear, she just determinedly pressed through each pedal stroke and continued on the route. The mechanic would ride up and see that she was in the wrong gear, either too high or too low. He would stop, park the van, and shift her bike into an appropriate gear for the terrain she was on.

On days when the mechanic bicycled, he would ride with her

and coach her on shifting. It seemed like she would have it mastered, yet the next day, the mechanic would drive up, see her pedaling in an inefficient gear, stop, and change it for her again. Later into the tour, she and I began cycling our days together. I truly enjoyed her company. We had lots of laughs at the silliest things. With my coaching, she finally seemed to master the need and ability to shift to be in an optimum gear for the varying terrain. Here is yet another example that it takes more determination than skill to bicycle coast to coast.

I believe that a mirror is essential, whether it is on the bike, helmet, visor, or glasses. Forrest Roberts used a dot mirror on his glasses. I could not adjust to using one of those. My preference is to have a mirror that clips to the visor of my helmet. Having it on the visor, rather than mounted on the frame of my glasses, sets it farther ahead of my eyes, which made it easier for me to adapt to. I know racers do not use visors, but racers do not even use mirrors. Besides being the mount for my mirror, I like having a visor to keep the sun off my face and for keeping the rain off my glasses.

Mine is not a racer's bike. In my handlebar bag I carry sunscreen, chamois cream, snack bars, trail mix, my camera, the bike cable lock, Wet Ones, pens, papers, maps, a handkerchief, a bandana, electrolyte capsules, Gatorade powder, maybe a sandwich, whatever. A waterproof or very water resistant route sheet or map holder is valuable. A cycle meter on the bike is mandatory for following the directions and knowing when to turn. The meter batteries must be able to power to the end of the trip.

Arriving at the Start

We have to make arrangements to be at the location the tour

company chooses for the start, and ensure that our bicycles are there. On all my rides, we convened and checked-in the day before the first day of cycling at a hotel. I usually box my bicycle and ship it two weeks before to the start. The tour organizers made arrangements with the hotel to accept the participants' boxed bikes. Sometimes, the tour organizers arranged that we could send our bicycle to a bike shop, where for a fee, they would assemble our bike.

A month before the trip, I take my bike to my local bike shop and tell them I want to ride it across the country. I have them true the wheels and inspect, lube, and tune the bike. They usually tell me of things that will make it safer or shift or stop better. After their adjustments, I ride it locally to ensure it is operating properly. If necessary, I have time to return it to them for further adjustments. I disassemble and box my own bike. I get the box from the bike shop. Others have the local shop disassemble and pack the bike. The local shop is also able to ship it as they have delivery trucks coming and going regularly. They either add the fees to my account or charge my credit card.

I usually ship my bike via United Parcel Service (UPS). Some prefer to ship via Federal Express. Others will bring their bicycles with them as luggage on the plane when they fly to the start. It used to cost $25 to ship a bicycle coast to coast via UPS. Their prices and Fed Ex's prices have been steeply rising. Now the expense is close to $80. Their fees vary by origination and destination zip codes and by the weight of the box. They now also tack on an oversize fee that sends the price way high. These ever increasing prices now match what is usually charged by the airlines to bring the boxed bicycle as luggage on the flight.

Hauling a big bike box along with seven weeks worth of travel luggage to and from the airport may be a challenge. On the other hand, bringing the bike as luggage on the plane, ensures that it is there as soon as I arrive. The risk of how airline staff handle the boxed bike is probably the same as how UPS or Fed Ex staff handle it. I do not know how the federal Transportation Security Agency (TSA) deals with boxed bicycles now. TSA will probably open the securely wrapped and taped box. It is probably best to not pack lots of other stuff in with the bike. That would make the TSA employee's job more difficult and may agitate him or her into being less careful repacking the machine, which I so carefully tried to protect and will be relying on for the next two months. These days, I would probably ship UPS or Fed Ex rather than stress over what TSA staff may decide to do.

Please know that the bicycle must be put in a box to bring it on an airline. On one of my tours, a cyclist called the airline to confirm that she could bring her bicycle with her on the flight. She was assured by her phone call that she could bring it on the flight with her. She was told that she could check it as an additional piece of luggage, but that she would have to pay an additional $80 for it as over-size luggage. She understood. They told her that she could bring it to the baggage check counter with her other bags on the day of her flight.

Having called ahead and having the assurances that she indeed could bring her bicycle with her on the plane, she walked through the airport terminal with her bags for her seven-week journey and rolled her assembled, ready-to-ride bicycle to the baggage check counter. She had not put it into a box. On the phone, the agent had never stated that the bicycle had to be in a box.

The cross-country cyclist was completely unprepared to hear from the check-in agent that she could not put her bike, as it was, on the plane. He kept saying that it had to be in a box. She kept saying that she had called ahead and they said she could just bring it. The clock was ticking to the flight's departure time.

The agent's supervisor was also insisting that the bike had to be in a box. The cyclist's emotional high of setting out for this adventurous coast-to-coast cycling tour was being driven to sullen lows. She continually heard that she could not bring her bicycle on the plane, although her expectations had been that she would. The airline staff eventually disclosed that crates exist for passenger's special needs. That glimmer of hope soon faded, as the staff could not locate any crates.

In this commotion at the baggage counter with the cyclist's emotions plunged to their lowest sub depths, another airline representative came to see what was happening. Amazingly, this airline person, who had authority, knew the cyclist from a neighborhood where they both had lived in years previous. This airline manager stepped in and rescued the cyclist. With just minutes before the scheduled departure time, a crate was located, the airline staff put the bike into the crate, and the cycling traveler boarded the plane in the last minutes to departure. Heroes and angels abound. True story!

Enjoy Your Venture

I do not think any cyclist sleeps much the night before they begin their first day of coast-to-coast pedaling. My things are never adequately organized for me to lie down early enough to have the hours of sleep I should have before my first long demanding ride.

For many, there are the jitters and nervousness of what it will be like and concern whether they can do it. Have they prepared adequately? How difficult will it be? Are they really ready? There are worries that everybody else will bicycle faster than they are able to and concerns that they will be left behind. There are fears that they will be alone, maybe get lost, maybe be abandoned with mechanical problems. Some worry that the tour staff will be angry that they must provide service to them. In my experience and observations, I say, "Relax!" There is a good chance that if you set a slower pace, in a few days, others will join you.

While on these tours, my bike is rarely cleaned. That is okay. There are cyclists on these trips who wipe their bicycle down every evening. They do not carry much gear on them or on their bicycles. They may have a small flat repair bag under their seat, but do not usually have extra bags on their bikes. They can and want to ride fast. Their bicycles are usually very expensive, lightweight machines. On the other hand, some folks pedal heavy bikes. Some of those fast cyclists probably would not ride one of those heavy bikes even one week nor even one eighty-five mile day.

Dave Fitton of Belleville, New Jersey had bicycled across the country on a previous Lung Association Big Ride. He returned in 2003 to repeat the tour. After he flew into Seattle, he shopped until he found and purchased a second-hand hybrid bicycle with upright handlebars. This is what he pedaled across the country.

He wore hiking boots when he rode. When he climbed in altitude and needed another layer for warmth, Dave wore blue jeans. He put a blue plastic milk crate on the back of his bike, and at the end of each day he would show us all the treasures that he had stopped to pick up, put into his basket, and brought to camp. There were lots of bungi cords, a doll with a missing eye, an orange Gumby pony, a perfectly functioning blue mini-mag light, tools, rope, gloves, shirts, hats, pens, pencils, a cuddly toy dog with cuts where its stuffing was puffing out. He picked up an inflatable, bright yellow, life-preserver rubber ducky that he wore around his waist on many days as he bicycled, which was noticed by the vehicle drivers. Dave show us all that these crossings should be fun.

If you are a slower cyclist, you may want to start your cycling earlier in the morning or spend much less time at the rest stops. Faster cyclists could perhaps slow down or spend more time at the rest stops or in the towns. The difference in pedaling speed is shown in the following Speed-Time Table. This table shows that at my average ten mph pace, I will be cycling eight hours to travel eighty miles. My comrades who can ride a fast sixteen mph average, only need five hours to travel those eighty miles; I never see those guys out on the road.

Average Speed	Time for One Mile	Time to Travel			
(mph)	(minutes per mile)	40 miles	60 miles	80 miles	100 miles
10 mph	6.0 min	4.0 hrs	6.0 hrs	8.0 hrs	10.0 hrs
12 mph	5.0 min	3.3 hrs	5.0 hrs	6.7 hr	8.3 hrs
14 mph	4.3 min	2.9 hrs	4.3 hrs	5.7 hrs	7.1 hrs
16 mph	3.8 min	2.5 hrs	3.8 hrs	5.0 hrs	6.3 hrs
18 mph	3.3 min	2.2 hrs	3.3 hrs	4.4 hrs	5.6 hrs

Happiness is being a bicycling family. It is best for us to bond from the beginning with other cyclists on the tour. Our moods fluctuate through a month of days. The adversities of bicycling all day and continually relocating create stress in others at different times for various reasons. We should develop camaraderie together against the common adversities, not against one another.

Rest days are scheduled for us to rest. We may have to skip the extended tour of the town, especially if we must take it by walking or bicycling. We must tend to bike maintenance. I need time to simply rest my body. Some cyclists spent a great part of the rest day disassembling and cleaning their bikes. Somehow, that guaranteed that we would be cycling in rain the next day or two. A few caught up with their journaling. Others wrote post cards. That was also a day to restock needed toiletry items if such stores were conveniently nearby to walk to. I need to arrange a fair distance of continuous walking into my day. My back, leg, ankle, knee, and foot muscles need a different motion from cycling. Walking mitigates pains that develop in my shins when I do not utilize muscles other than those for cycling. On rest days, it was good not be on the bike, although many rode those days too, at least a little.

Massage is excellent for relieving our stressed muscles. If we can afford the service, it is a perfect thing to do on our rest days. With the long distance cycling of the cross-country rides, I must limit my massages to only one section of my body – either legs or back, shoulders, and arms – per session. A full body massage leave me too exhausted to complete the following day's demanding ride. The nap I need to restore my energy usually does not fit the schedule. TK&A provided a masseuse on their staff. She was most always working late into the evenings and all day on our rest days.

Perfect Fit

I am certainly not an expert on bicycling fitness and conditioning and must refer you to Bicycling Magazine and the many Bicycling Magazine books published by Rodale Inc. for excellent information. Three of my favorite books are Bicycling Magazine's <u>1000 All-Time</u>

Best Tips edited by Ben Hewitt, Bike For Life - How to Ride to 100 by Roy M. Wallock and Bill Katovsky, and Bicycling Magazine's The Complete Book of Long-Distance Cycling by Edmund R. Burke, Ph.D. and Ed Pavelka. Since you have read this far, however, I suppose that I could offer some tips that seem to be most needed by my bicycling friends. I do have many hours of experience that may be helpful. These are my opinions. I am not a physiology expert. You may need to modify these tips for your body shape and condition.

Be sure to have a comfortable bicycle that fits you and make the necessary adjustments to optimize the fit. Following are some thoughts that have worked for me. If you have physical limitations or pain with these recommendations, you will need to make modifications. You may want to seek advice from a professional bicycle fitter or a physical therapy specialist.

Set the cleats of your shoes so that the balls of your feet are over the pedal axles. As you pedal, your knees should move up and down in-line with the pedals. They should not be bowlegged. Your feet should be slightly pigeon-toed by rotating your heels out. Setting the cleats on your shoes to the best position may require several tedious readjustments. Some say that problems they had with their toes going numb were alleviated after they made adjustments to their cleats.

The top of your saddle should be level. I adjust this with the bike on a level surface and eye the top of the saddle, nose to tail, along some horizontal line to the side of the saddle. If the nose is raised, you may have pain when you lean forward. When the nose is too low, the tendency is to put more weight than you should on your hands. Remember, use your abdominal muscles to hold your torso.

Position your pelvis on the widest part of the saddle while sitting upright or leaning forward slightly. Place the bottoms of the back of your feet on the pedals. You want the saddle height high enough that you can straighten your legs as you pedal, but your hips should not be rocking from side to side.

Another saddle adjustment is setting its forward or backward location. Position the bottom of your pelvis bone on the saddle and put the balls of your feet on the pedals placed horizontal at the 3:00 and 9:00 positions. A weighted string can help you determine if the position of your forward knee is directly above the pedal axle. Hold the weighted string just below the kneecap, at the indented part. The string should drop down in line with the pedal axle. With time and patience you will have your saddle fitted properly. Once you have done all that, wrap two or three turns of black electrical tape around the seat post at and just above where it fits into the seat tube to mark your seat height adjustment.

Next test your reach to the handlebars. Rest your hands on the top horizontal sides of your handlebars with your arms bent. You should not be able to see the front wheel axle because the handlebars should obstruct your view of it. Adjustments for your reach will require purchasing a longer or shorter stem. Work with your local bike shop to find a good fitting stem. Remind them that you are not a racer and may need to modify the optimum reach.

Another note to prevent pinching the nerves in your wrists: it is recommended to ride with your hands positioned on the sides of the handlebars so that your fingers are to the outer side and your thumbs are on the inner sides. Having your wrists folded outward as when your hands are placed nearer to the centers of the bars, with your fingers wrapped above the bars and your thumbs below the bars, has been suspected of developing carpal tunnel syndrome in the wrists.

Now that you have your bicycle perfectly fitted to you, ride. Pedal with your knees above the pedals, your feet slightly pigeon-toed, and your back straight. Perfect your spinning. Pull up. Scuff forward at the top. Push down. Scuff backward at the bottom. Use your abdominal muscles to hold your torso, keep your neck in line with your spine, and stretch out your spine. Relax your shoulder blades down your back. Tilt the bottom of your pelvis forward and under to keep the bone on the saddle. Use your abdominal muscles as the core of your strength. Use the strength in your legs. Spin. Relax. Breathe. And when you see me, remind me of all these things.

Climb hills. Take on headwinds. Ride out with a tailwind and exert yourself on the return. Push yourself to exhaustion. Your fatigue will make it harder, exactly the conditioning for what you will be experiencing on your cross-country ride. Do it again the next day or at least take an easy ride the next day.

Bicycle Care

When you park your bicycle, it is best to lean it against a wall, post, tree, or other solid vertical structure with the derailleur side toward the solid surface. If your bike falls, there is less risk of damaging the derailleur. It is depressing how sometimes other people, even cyclists, will knock your bike over. Sometimes the wind surprisingly sends it away. It is also good practice to lean the saddle against the wall. Sometimes when the bike is leaning on the handlebars, the front will pivot and the bike will fall. Do not lean your bike on any vehicle; too often the bike will fall and scratch the car.

If there is no place to lean it, you will have to lay it down. Lay it with the derailleur side up. Position the left pedal to the rear, between the chain stay and the seat stay, so that the rear of the bike rests on the pedal, rather than on the frame or the quick-release lever. Turn the handlebars to the

right as far as they will go so that the weight of the front of the bike is on the front tire-rolling surface; then the handlebars will stay off the ground. The third point of contact will be the saddle.

Ensure that the wheel quick-release skewers are tight. Previously I had these over-tightened. I have since been advised of a better method of setting the correct tension. The proper tightness is achieved by starting with the quick-release lever straight out, in line with the axle. Tighten the nut at the other end finger tight. I tip the quick-release lever backward a bit to compensate for my female and aging strength. Tighten the nut a bit more and then close the lever. Unless you have a more expensive quick-release lever, it should be hard to push closed.

For each wheel, pick the bike up and spin the wheel. Ensure that it spins freely and that the brakes are not dragging on it.

On our central crossing, Neil Sardiñas from King of Prussia, Pennsylvania gave us a great tip for putting a chain back on when it comes off the inside of the granny gear cog. Stand at the side of the bike opposite the side of the chain. Put the bottom front of your shoe up by the bottom bracket. With the toe of your shoe, locate and push the chain down and on to the cog-set; then rotate the pedals backward pulling the chain back on over the cog. This is a slick and quick way to put that chain back on without getting chain lube on your fingers. I recommend putting a device called a Third Eye Chain Watcher on your bike to prevent that chain from ever coming off the inside of the granny gear. If your chain repeatedly comes off to the inside of the granny gear, you need to have your shifter mechanically adjusted.

Tour Group or Solo

Some cyclists attempt the cross-country journey by themselves or with one other person. I do not think that I would ever want to do that. A year's worth of research is needed before ever starting the trip. They have to determine which roads to travel. The Adventure Cycling Association of Missoula, Montana has many maps available that help with this, although there will always be sections where the traveler would have to fill in details. The cyclists would have to determine how far to bicycle each day and determine how their desired distance fits in with the overnight places. All the lodging has to be arranged. Whether staying at motels or at campgrounds, lots of phone calls have to be made for reservations. They have to carry all that contact information. Complex mechanical issues with their bicycles have to be handled without the luxury of a support vehicle. Across the Great Plains, the distance to a bike shop that could fix it may be hundreds of miles away, and not necessarily in the direction they had planned to go.

On our twenty-seventh day of the Southern Crossing Tour, Steve Bryant of Cypress, California experienced the disappointment of a broken bicycle frame. It had broken where the rear wheel axle and derailleur attach, where the seat stay and the chain stay meet. The same place where mine had broken; it must be a vulnerable place on a bike frame. Steve cleverly devised a patch so that he could continue cycling for the day; however, he knew that the kludge would not hold together very long. The next day, while our cycling group continued our eastbound journey from Edna to Freeport, Texas, the TK&A staff drove Steve and his bicycle north to Houston. The Specialized bicycle dealer there honored the warranty and exchanged bikes with Steve. He acquired a brand new bike and was back cycling with us the following day. Bicycling across the country without the support and assistance of a tour organization could make breakdowns particularly disheartening. A solo cyclist could rely on the kindness of strangers and eventually resolve complications. Steve, however, was on vacation and was grateful for the help from the knowledgeable TK&A staff.

You may want to bike across the country, but have doubts that group touring would be suitable for you. You may believe that the support provided would be indispensable, but think the average daily distance are too extreme. Call the tour company, and discuss with them your concerns. Query whether they will allow you to ride in the SAG vehicle if you do not want to ride the entire day's distance. Since you would be paying them, they should. You may need to ride in the SAG vehicle to heal and that should be okay with the tour staff. Perhaps you want to bike some every day, but just cannot bear the extended distances day after day after day. Tell the SAG van driver you want a lift. You will still be seeing and experiencing a large part of the country via bicycle. You may be surprised how many miles you can travel by bicycle when the pressure to go fast and the worry of the overall distance is removed.

Organization's Planning

The planning a tour organization does for a coast-to-coast tour is probably far more extensive than one would initially think. For each day, they must list the exact distance to each turn. The mileage must be accurate with every left, right, and crossing from the first pedal of the morning to the last pedal at the next overnight location. Also, landmarks, convenience stores, and restaurants are noted with the distance to them. The directions and turn-by-turn mileages must be correctly and tediously typed. A turn or mileage can easily be offset while typing, but has major impact on the cyclist's travel.

Copies for each of the thirty or more cyclists for all fifty or so days must be printed out. The many paper copies of the route directions for each cyclist have to be carried in the SAG van to each new location when that day's guide sheets are given to the cyclists.

The tour company must call and reserve lodging and food and facilities for thirty or more ravenous cyclists and staff. The company has to determine which size of vehicles to send to accommodate the cyclists, their duffels, and other gear. Willing staff to support the cyclists must be located. Finding a willing and able mechanic for the low or non-paying two-month expedition can be difficult.

The tour company must obtain and pay for insurances. Tour staff must handle pre-trip phone calls and paper work for the participants. From the office, staff explain concerns and answer questions from the cyclists. How to bring gear to the start? How to get home after? How to transport the bike case? Is their bike okay for the trip? What pre-trip bike maintenance should be done? Will they be capable of doing the ride? What should be packed? How can their family contact them? How much money will be needed?

The tour organization must locate SAG stops at the correct and needed distance. Sometimes finding a location with tables, shade, and toilets can be a challenge. The staff haul out water, sports drinks, snacks, bananas, etc. for the cyclists. Staff stay there (sometimes for hours) while the first through the last cyclists come in for their rest, hydration, and nourishment. The tours I traveled with also requested that each cyclist sign-in when they arrived so that staff had assurance that each person had arrived to that location.

Many of the tour groups have someone drive the route weeks before the cyclists begin and update the daily route sheets before printing copies enough for each cyclist. Sometimes road construction forces a change to the route.

Be prepared to tip the tour staff. On many of the lower priced trips, staff members are not paid by the tour organization. The individuals provide staff services because they love the sport. Perhaps, for them it is a working vacation and an inexpensive way to travel. When you consider the cost of the tour and the trip, allocate an additional two percent to tip the staff for all the services they provide. The staff will be heaving your luggage, placing it with care, and treating it gently. They provide the snacks, set up the rest stops, track that you are on route and safe out there on the bike, and cheer you on.

Driving the SAG vehicle while simultaneously navigating and following the directions, which are designed for bicycling, is a challenge. Often the signs are more difficult to read when other vehicles force swift movement. It is even more confusing and difficult following the route sheet in the opposite direction.

Because staff are tending to the needs of all the cyclists, their days will be the longest. Tour staff will probably be the first up in the morning and the last to sleep every night. They usually take the job for the love of the sport and not for the money, because it usually pays nearly nothing. The demands of staff members' time, skill, and labor are extensive. When one cyclist is hurt, the staff must tend to this person and still tend to the needs of the other cyclists. It is a long, exhausting trip for them, just as it is for the cyclist.

The support vehicle and support staff are there for you. If your bicycling experience is being miserable, take the lift in the SAG van. Take the pressure off yourself. This is your vacation. Have some fun. The staff should be supportive and never use diminutive nor derogatory comments when the last straws of the demands of the trip weigh too heavily on you. Tour staff should never make it seem like they are annoyed that you want to ride in the support vehicle. You paid them and they are there to support you. It amazes me when I hear stories of support staff that give these negative attitudes to the cyclists. I have always had great support staff and hope that when I am providing the support, my cyclists find me encouraging, supportive, and their biggest fan.

No Expectations

Some have a goal to bicycle every inch. They proudly proclaim to belong to the every inch club. Some have infirmities such as knee problems, saddle sores, or illness that remove them from the membership. As for me, I do not think continuous climbing along the shoulder of Interstate-80, while cars and trucks howl by at eighty-five miles per hour spraying me with dirty, gritty, cold rain is how I want to spend my vacation. There is a big, warm van ready and willing to load my bike and zip me up this mountain range to the dry hotel. Those days, when the van rescued me, allowed my body to rest. It was pleasant to be into the overnight facility and have time to explore it. Then I had time to relax and talk with the faster cyclists that I cannot ride with and rarely have the opportunity of talking with.

"No expectations!" is a good rule. Often even the tour staff do not know what will be found along the route or at the day's final destination. Just when we long to have something along the route or at the end, near the overnight location, we find ourselves cycling in forever wilderness or lodging at a site far away from the town and conveniences. We had to learn to take the ride as it comes. It is what it is. Have no expectations. Be open and aware to the subtle treats. They will be sweeter when they are not expected.

So Go

Here are my suggestions for those who take the leap and set out on a coast-to-coast crossing. Do not allow yourself to be caught up in what seems to be demanding hastiness. The bicycling is very demanding. Packing up your gear every day and relocating elicits its arduous demands. It is not necessary to bike fast or be quick on the climbs. Gear down. Relax your upper body. Use your abdominal muscles to hold your torso. Keep your legs going, but look up and look around. These coast-to-coast bicycling ventures connect us to nature. Just as animals and birds migrate, some of us need to migrate. Enjoy the scenery; watch the inches roll away. Take in the sights: the vegetation, the rocks, the mountains, the birds, the sky, and the clouds.

Be where you are. You will never be at that place, under those circumstances, with those people, again, ever. In my opinion, making the most and the best of where you are is your most precious purpose. Dispel any concern about where you will end the day or about arriving there at some particular time. Do not be concerned that another cyclist is ahead of you or that you have to catch up or keep up with them. The faster cyclist could slow his or her pace a bit to create a sociable cycling experience. So maybe you could arrive a half hour sooner. Then what? Your life is here and now, bicycling across the country.

Watch the local people as you go by and wave to them. Become aware of what is occupying their day. Wave to drivers. Sending them a friendly message may make a difference in how they pass the next cyclist: perhaps more slowly or allowing more space between their vehicle and the cyclist. If a driver gives a nasty gesture, do not add to it. Do not perpetuate what you do not like. Let it stop with you. Ask the angels to handle that driver's issues. Return a friendly gesture to them. Try it.

Be observant of the nature that surrounds you. When you are cycling and talking with other cyclists, remember to look around. Look for the prairie dogs popping out of their holes. Behold the life around you. Watch for the hawks perched on the utility poles. If you pay attention, perhaps you will observe a hawk swoop down and snatch up a squirrel. You are traveling at the perfect pace to allow the nuances of nature to permeate into your essence, where they may penetrate to your mind and emotions. Concentrate on your cycling, but look around so you also see the haunted house with vines growing all over, which others will be talking about after the ride. Do not miss joining in the excitement with your friend on the bicycle behind you as he revels in seeing the sleek, muscular, black snake climbing a tree. They do not have opposing thumbs. They do not even have hands and legs. How can they climb a tree? Stop occasionally to look back on the miles you have come and the places you have been.

It is a Big Country

There will be times when you have already been on the bike for many hours. You will be tired. Your body will ache. Perhaps saddle sores will be irritating you. Perhaps a blazing, hot sun is scorching and dehydrating you. Stay optimistic. Too soon it will all be over. You are now on a wondrous adventure that few others have the courage to undertake. This is your vacation of a lifetime. Make it one that you will treasure, long remember, and want to relive in your mind. Breathe. Draw the air in deep. Treasure your vigor and vitality. Cherish another day of good health to be out here doing such a silly thing as just riding your bicycle. Smile. Wave to someone.

Link up with another cyclist. Find ten things to compliment

them on. Tell them one or two of those compliments as you spark up your conversation with them. Encourage them to tell you something that you did not know. Whatever the conditions, you are sharing the experience with those other cyclists. Let yourself be motivated by and bond with your co-cyclists.

It is what it is. Yeah, it is hot. Yeah, you are pushing into a strong headwind. Be grateful for that modern bicycle you have and its many gears. Coast-to-coast cycling teaches tolerance. Adopt the attitude of no expectations.

Appreciate the vastness of this country. Get out of yourself. Expand your anchor points. Extend your senses beyond just that road, beyond that field. Reach to the expansive mountains and beyond to the horizon. Take in the sky and the clouds. What things do the clouds make you think of?

In the vast open lands, think about what living there would be like. What would it have been like centuries ago before modern machinery? What would it have been like to live there when Kokopeli roamed from tribe to tribe? What would life have been like for those who lived in cliff walls?

If you were a talented artist and could recreate those surrounding landscapes with brushes on a canvas, what whimsical liberties might you add? Do you picture and would you paint wolves, dinosaurs, or spaceships? Can you envision a secluded, modern American Dream home with a hangar for your personal airplane next to your private runway? Let your mischievous imagination free to play.

Give thanks for your blessings. Be grateful for your health. Realize how rich you are to be out here on your fine bicycle. Celebrate that you have all that you have. Celebrate your friends, your family, your home, your job, your income, your vision, your co-cyclists sharing these experiences, and the tour staff that is assisting you. Rejoice in this vast country that you are experiencing. Acknowledge your determination. Persevere. You are the hero.

Some cyclists love to come in early and swim. I have never been excited about swimming, and I never thought I was missing much at the pool. Some come in and nap. Sometimes when I am exhausted and in need of a nap, I am still many miles from the end of the day's ride. When I can find surroundings that are pleasant and I need a nap, I will take one mid route. I have had concerned motorists stop and ask whether I was okay. It was an opportunity to let them know that I was just resting from my many miles that morning and the many days since I pedaled away from the ocean waters. I love having that opportunity to talk with them.

Keep on Spinning

These cross-country rides are a trade-off between time and money. Seven weeks is a long time to not be bringing in a paycheck. Many think that they cannot be away from their jobs for seven consecutive weeks. Some think that they are irreplaceable. Others think that the employer would not give them that much time off even without pay. Maybe they are wrong.

There are few other countries in the world that are as vast as the United States and are also covered by many smooth and wide road surfaces. When Andy Hiroshima of Sacramento, California told his friend that he was going to bicycle across the country, his friend suggested that he may want to choose a smaller country.

Bicycling coast to coast is for those people who live an active lifestyle and desire an active vacation. Although it is very challenging, it is more rewarding than many other kinds of adventures. Engaging and physically demanding the performance of your body rewards your mind and soul. The experience will be more memorable because of your achievements. You will develop tight bonds of friendship with your cycling tour companions as you overcome the adversities together. Give thanks for your health, your abilities, and your physical gifts, and use them.

Should you choose to venture a cross-country ride, be confident that you can do it. Determine whether or not your goal is to pedal every inch. It never was for me. One of the wonderful things about bicycling is how you will be able to just keep rolling a little bit farther. Even easy pressure on your legs and pedals will keep you progressing along. This is your chance to delight in your health and your blessings and experience wherever you currently are in this great nation. Think of what history the area has to tell.

I would like to pedal across the United States again. I would take more time to stop and talk with local people along the route. Being able to bicycle faster may allow me to stop longer and absorb more of the flavor of the community and the pulse of the peoples' lives. Many of the faster cyclists that I have pedaled with tend to get caught up in the "going faster." Sometimes I do, too. They seem to concentrate so much on their cycling speed that they do not slow down when they come into a town or neighborhood. My preference is to see what is there. I often take side trips through communities to see the surroundings, find what local activities are occurring, and read the information on historical markers.

The experience of the cross-country journey permeates our lives and expands our horizons. The journey is embedded into our memories and into our essence. When we recall the tour, we recall the richness of having been there. We are grateful for the experience, and we remember our being most alive.

I hope this book will inspire those who are dreaming and longing to take action to bicycle from sea to shining sea. Sign up. Do it. Delight in your physical, mental, and spiritual vigor and vitality. Cherish your enthusiasm. Keep on spinning. Enjoy the ride.